Academic Heraldry in America

Academic Heraldry in America

KEVIN SHEARD, J. D.

Illustrations by PAUL WAINIO

NORTHERN MICHIGAN COLLEGE PRESS
Marquette, Michigan

T H E B O O K C O N C E R N

Hancock, Michigan

Printed in the U.S.A.

To

Josephine E. and the late Thomas D. Phillips

OF MARIETTA COLLEGE

A N D

IN RECOGNITION OF WHAT I HAVE RECEIVED

E LIBERALITATE E. WILLIAMS ARMIGERI

$f$oreword

THIS BOOK like many others is the result of an unsatisfied curiosity. It was a well known "fact" that every college has a hood which is unique in the design of its lining. In theory when one sees a hood he can identify the college or university which awarded it. Since the number of schools in the country makes it impossible to remember all of the designs, obviously there should be a book wherein the information can be found. Casting about for such a book I found only an outdated and inaccurate one which provided no way of proceeding from an unknown hood to the institution which awarded it. I then turned to robemakers and discovered that they were unable or unwilling to provide any lists. The conclusion followed that were any such book to be made available I should have to write it myself. The practical problem of financing was solved only when the Northern Michigan College Foundation agreed to subsidize the gathering of information. For this I shall always be grateful.

The increasing numbers of both institutions and students in recent years has led to a greater interest in academic heraldry than ever before. As more and more of our young people earn degrees and gain the right to wear academic costume and to partake in the ceremonies which are part of the educational tradition, more and more questions are asked. Perhaps, however, the interest is not universal. In a suburb of Boston, the great mother of American colleges today looks with "affable tolerance" on "academic haberdashery." This is reflected in the Spartan simplicity of its recently adopted code which permits only a black tassel to be worn on the cap which appears over the crimson gown decorated with colored crow's feet to indicate the faculty. At any rate, this book is intended to satisfy the curiosity of the others.

As the project developed it became apparent that there was interest in phases of academic heraldry other than hoods. As a result the scope was expanded until the book reached its present form.

It should be noted at the outset that the word "heraldry" is used in a popular sense rather than in any technical one. As a lover of the ancient science I should be the first to admit that this work violates many of the rules of classical heraldry. Yet, because the problems in the area of academic insignia are similar to those in armory, I have not hesitated to use the same vocabulary where appropriate. At the same time I have not seen fit to retain the limitations of ancient heraldry. I trust my friends among the armorialists will not be offended.

The methodology of this study was simple. Every degree-granting institution in the United States listed in the *Education Directory* of the Office of Education was approached by mail. Each was asked to complete a form giving details on its hood and the precedence date used by the school. After a reasonable time all those colleges and universities which grant higher degrees and had not answered the first request were approached again. The third step was to write personal letters to the presidents of nationally known institutions which had not responded to either of the other appeals. As a result the only unverified hood descriptions in the book are those of certain of the constituent elements of the State University of New York. They were obtained from trustworthy outside sources.

The material on ceremonies, seals, and flags is of necessity general and not susceptible of verification. It is based on close acquaintance with many schools and reasonable familiarity with many others.

This book was at first intended to be a simple report. I found it impossible, however, to avoid making evaluations and suggestions when, for example, the number of duplications of hood designs was discovered. All such non-factual matters have, I think, been plainly indicated as being my own by the language used.

I acknowledge with gratitude the work of the presidents, vice-presidents, registrars, and other officials who took the time to answer my requests for information. Thanks are due for the assistance of Professors Roy E. Heath and Luther S. West of the Research Committee of Northern Michigan College who so ably forwarded the cause of the subsidy and to Dr. Earl R. Hilton for checking the manuscript. I should also make special mention of the encouragement of Professor Albert B. Cook III, whose enthusiasm for the project so often exceeded my own.

KEVIN SHEARD
Northern Michigan College

$\mathcal{C}$ontents

Page

Academic Costume in America 1

Faculty Colors 7

Hood Designs 8

Hood Lining Colors 9

Hoods - Institutions Table 10

Institutions—Hoods Table 35

Non - Code Hoods 65

Academic Processions 69

The Commencement Ceremony 71

Academic Seals 73

Academic Flags 74

Bibliography 77

Abbreviations

A	Agricultural
C	College
Ch.	Chevron (Point Up)
Ch. Rev.	Chevron Reversed (Point Down)
Cons.	Conservatory
Ed	Education
Inst	Institute or Institution
M	Mechanic Arts or Mechanical
Sch	School
Sem	Seminary
St	State or Saint
SUNY	State University of New York, used to identify constituent elements, all of which have individual names.
Tchrs	Teachers
Tech	Technology or Technological
Theo	Theology or Theological
U	University

Academic Heraldry in America

Academic Costume in America

J UST BEFORE the beginning of the twentieth century it seemed that colleges and universities in the United States were developing the kind of ruleless academic costume that emerged from the centuries in Great Britain. There and in the dominions each university adopted its own costume without regard to what other institutions had done. The result is a confusing array of caps, gowns, and particularly hoods, each one of which must be separately memorized.

Made aware of the problem by the writings of G. C. Leonard, American institutions responded by sending representatives to a commission in 1895 to consider a uniform code for academic costume. The deliberations of the group produced the system which is still in use today, although slightly modified by successor committees appointed by the American Council on Education. The latest of these groups met in 1959.

The code has three main parts; that is, it deals with caps, gowns, and hoods. Of these the caps are the simplest. Although there is an exception, rarely seen, for women which allows them to wear a soft cap, the mortarboard or Oxford type cap is worn. At this point, remote in time from the deliberations, it seems unfortunate that the commission did not adopt the alternate possibility open to it, based on the Cambridge model. This is a soft cap which resembles an overlarge beret. It is more comfortable than the Oxford type and is much more functional without any loss in dignity. Be that as it may, the mortarboard is apparently here to stay. It is always black and may be of an appropriate material except that velvet is reserved to doctors.

The tassel worn with the cap has three variations. First, it may be black for any degree. Second, it may be in the color of the faculty in which the degree was granted. (The word "faculty" as used here means a major field of learning such as Arts, Law, or Philosophy.) The colors associated with each faculty are given below. The third area of choice in the tassel is restricted to doctors and governing officials of institutions. These groups alone may wear one made of gold metallic thread. There are two other practices which should be mentioned because, although outside of the code, they are in use in a few institutions. One is using the tassel to indicate academic honors. At the University of Wisconsin, for example, all candidates for bachelors' degrees wear black tassels except for those who will be graduated with honors. They wear one which is red and white. The practice has little to recommend it, but if it is followed the special tassel should be displayed for the one day only. That is, it should not be a lifetime costume for the honors graduate. The other deviation is to use a tassel which is half blue and half pink to indicate a degree in Music Education. Carried to its logical conclusion this would require the holder of a degree in the History of Church Music and Art to wear three colors and so on.

Some discussion has been engendered about the proper side of the mortarboard on which to wear the tassel. The 1959 committee of the American Council on Education recommends that it be permitted to lie where it will. The group, however, recognizes that in some schools a ceremony is made of switching the tassel from the right to the left at the moment the degree is awarded. It is suggested that this is a substitute for individual hooding of candidates. It must be added that this is a very poor substitute since the first gust of wind is likely to deprive the new Bachelor of Arts of the symbol of his degree. A common practice for doctors, at least, is to sew the tassel in place.

One last comment on tassels seems to be in order. They are frequently made and worn in a length that is downright uncomfortable. There is no particular joy in being buffeted by a collection of strands that hang halfway down the side of the head. A more sensible rule would be to have all tassels cut to the two and one-half inches from the edge of the cap which is common among doctors' gold ones. Whether the shorter length is dictated by the cost of the gold is not at issue; it is simply easier on the wearer to have them short.

Gowns, which according to the code are all black, aside from variations in materials and fullness are of three kinds. The bachelor's gown is a relatively simple kind falling in straight lines from a fairly elaborate yoke. Its distinguishing characteristic is the long pointed sleeves. It should have no adornment although a few institutions pipe the yoke with a school color.

Masters' gowns until 1960 were set apart by a peculiar arrangement of the long sleeves whereby the arm emerged from the sleeve through a slit at the elbow. The rest of the sleeve dangled and terminated around the knee of the wearer in a square end into which a semi-circle was cut. The gown was the despair of the wearers because no matter how hot the day a coat had to be worn under it. Disregard of the rule led on occasion to spectacular, if incorrect results when members of the physical education department wearing short sleeved shirts were observed with their brawny arms protruding from the slits. In 1960, however, the gown was modified by the committee of the American Council on Education. In place of the elbow slit, an opening was made at the wrist and the gown was made to close. This ended the battle of the arms. Of course if one wears the old style master's gown, which may with propriety be done until it is no longer fit for wear, he should wear a coat.

The doctor's gown is an elaborate costume marked by velvet panels down the front and around the neck as well as by three bars of the same material on the bell shaped sleeves. It is cut much fuller than the other gowns and unlike them may be ornamented in color. Both the panelling and the sleeve bars may show the faculty in which the degree was awarded. As a matter of practice, however, except in the areas of Philosophy and Law, dark blue and purple, respectively, faculty colors are rarely seen on the gown. The reason seems to be that it is felt that other colors produce a garish effect.

Interestingly, although there is considerable variation among the non-code hoods, the standard cap and gown are almost universally worn. The only outstanding deviations are in the cases of Harvard, Princeton, and Yale. The first permits a crimson doctor's gown, the second allows blue for both masters and doctors, while the school colors of Princeton are shown by giving the doctors a typical black gown and then ornamenting it with orange "hashmarks" and sleeve linings. Harvard has one other relevant peculiarity. It is on her gowns, of all degrees, that she shows the faculty. Worked into the lapel is a crow's foot in the faculty color. It is double for earned degrees and triple for honoraries.

A few schools use gowns for all instructional periods. Villa Madonna College, for example, prescribes them for all faculty members who are not habitually dressed in the garments of religious orders. Aside from the symbolism, the gown has the advantage of keeping chalk dust in one place. In this sense the use resembles that of the shop coat.

While the code does not deal with academic costume of institutions on a level below that of the four year college, it does take cognizance of the fact that some junior schools do wear a costume. It recommends that such institutions use light colored gowns rather than black. Thus teacher training institutions are asked to use light blue and others to use light gray.

Of all the components of the costume the hood bears the heaviest symbolic burden. Since the cap, gown, and hood are no longer required to keep the wearer warm, their function is one of identification. To perform this they must make clear the level of the degree, the faculty in which it was given, and the institution which awarded it. The cap performs none of these tasks except to the extent that the velvet material marks the doctor and the tassel may show either the level by being made of gold thread or the faculty by being of some color. Since a doctor may wear a cap which is not made of velvet and anyone may elect to wear a black tassel, there is no certainty in the cap. Likewise the gown merely points out the level of the degree, not the institution which awarded it. To the extent that doctors use the velvet panelling and sleeve bars in color some information may be gleaned about the faculty.

It is on the hood alone that all three items are clearly shown. The level of the degree is shown by the size of the hood, the width of the velvet trimming, and, in the case of doctors, by the shape. The bachelor's, master's, and doctor's hoods are three feet, three and one-half feet, and four feet long, respectively. The velvet trimming in the same order is two, three and five inches. This extends all around the hood on the exposed edge. To make a more comfortable fit, it is allowed to narrow on the neck band.

This same trimming identifies the faculty in which the degree was awarded. For each faculty there is a corresponding color so a glance at the trimming is all that is needed to identify the faculty. A full list of the colors is given at the end of this section, but for purposes of illustration it may be said that White is used for Arts and Letters. Thus a Bachelor of Arts will wear a hood trimmed with a two inch White velvet border. The Master of Arts will have a three inch, and the Doctor of Letters a five inch White trim.

The unofficial practice of splitting the trimming to show two different faculties on one hood has always been frowned on, but in the report of the committee of 1959 it was definitely condemned. It may now be said that it is contrary to the code.

One change introduced by the report of the 1959 committee is of considerable importance and bears stressing. Formerly in the case of a degree of Bachelor of Science in Engineering the code called for a border of Yellow for Science rather than one of Orange for Engineering. In other words the faculty in which the work was actually done was ignored for a nominal one. Today the code requires the Orange in such a case. It could be argued that the difference is not very great, but where the degree is Bachelor of Science in Art, the Yellow trimming is inappropriate.

Unfortunately the ruling just mentioned does not clear up all difficulties. There is still the problem of such combinations as Bachelor of Music Education which were discussed under tassels. Further there are the degrees where the faculty is not really mentioned. For example, the writer has the degree of Master of Science for which he would wear the Yellow of science. To others it comes as a surprise to learn that his field was history. Here, perhaps the problem is not one of academic costume, but rather of the wording of the degree.

The last of the references in the hood is to the institution which awarded the degree or of which the wearer is a faculty member. The latter possibility should become rarer since the 1959 committee disapproved the practice of wearing the hood of an institution which did not award his degree. If an institution really wants its faculty to carry its hood it might possibly revert to the old custom of awarding degrees *ad eundem gradum*.

The commission of 1895 undertook to solve the problem of identifying the university in an ingenious way. It provided that the hood be lined with the colors of each school awarding degrees. In this manner a glance at the lining, which is worn exposed, would give the required information. In theory the method was simple. In practice, however, the sheer number of schools made it complex. With the growth of higher education and the consequent increase in the number of institutions the difficulties have multiplied. Obviously only a limited number of institutions can have single colors in the hoods. Although the spectrum has an infinite number of points, there are limits to the human ability to recognize them. Nevertheless it is difficult to understand why a school would deliberately adopt a hood lined only with "Yale Blue," thus becoming in effect an imitation Yale. To meet the need for further differentiation, two-color patterns were introduced and a registry system set up. Whatever the intentions of the commission, the overwhelming majority of schools has adopted the chevron design. A glance at the tables will show that this concentration has produced hundreds of duplicate hoods. The same thing is true to a lesser extent of other two-color designs. To make the situation worse some institutions have adopted two or even three hoods using one for Arts degrees and the others for Science and Education degrees, or making one represent earned degrees and the other or others represent honorary ones. There seems to be little justification for these practices because all recipients of degrees from a given institution are equally children of the Alma Mater and should have an equal right to bear her hood. As a practical matter traffic on what designs are available is unnecessarily congested.

A new look at the problem of giving each school its own distinctive hood shows that it is not insoluble. Certain assumptions on which to proceed are almost self evident. First, academic hoods are not coats of arms. Thus many of the limitations which exist in classical heraldry are not relevant. There is no need to limit colors to seven nor need the tincture rule, which forbids gold and silver to be used with or on one another, be taken seriously. Needless to say, the other part of the tincture rule which says that a charge of one color cannot be laid on another would be insupportable.

Second, while a vocabulary drawn from classic heraldry may be useful, since it faced a similar problem, there is no point in adopting the complications which go with it. The distinction between chevrons and chevronels has already been abolished in academic heraldry. It is proposed that diminutives of all other ordinaries used be similarly disregarded. This would lead to fess, bars, barrulets and others being known simply as bars. This even necessarily leads to the strange looking "party per bar." The alternative would be the even stranger looking "two fesses" which, incidentally, would be retaining a word not in the vocabulary of the average wearer of academic costume. Pale would include pallets.

Third, common charges are not suitable for differencing hoods since they would be lost in the folds.

Fourth, lines other than straight ones would cause difficulties in constructing hoods.

Illustrated are various hood designs which could be adopted. (The pictures are schematic rather than photographic.) Some of the designs are in use, although, except for the chevron, on a very limited scale. Each design is numbered to facilitate classification of hoods.

The designs are set out by families. It will be observed that the difference between two and three chevrons on the one hand and double and triple on the other lies in the fact that in the latter group the color of the field or background does not show between the chevrons. The same thing is true of bars and pales. In no case does the "double" refer to the height or width of the charge. In so far as Checky and Lozengy are concerned practical considerations of expense in construction may rule them out. There are, however, in current use two tartans which can be no less costly. If it is thought that checky and lozengy are too gaudy, a glance at the national arms of Monaco or Bavaria will be reassuring.

In describing a hood the background or field should be given first and then the number, color, and kind of charges (Light Blue, Three Gold Chevrons Reversed). Where the charge is between two colors the upper or left should be stated, then the charge, and finally the lower or right (Crimson, Gold Pale, Green). Where necessary to use further description, the words "top" and "bottom" should be employed in preference to "chief" and "base." The latter pair have been used only because in the past some have regarded the hood as an inverted shield. It was this straining of heraldic terminology which led to calling a point-down figure a chevron. (The usage is too well fixed to do anything about it now. It will simply have to be accepted that point-down is a chevron and point-up is a chevron reversed.) Right and left will be used to describe position. Since the hood is seen from the back and the observer's right and left are the same as the wearer's, there is no need to use "dexter" and "sinister."

It is proposed that any school which finds that it is using a hood common to other institutions consider changing to one of the other designs illustrated. The writer, who may be addressed at the Northern Michigan College Press, Marquette, Michigan, will be most appreciative of being informed of any changes. Further, he will be happy to cooperate with any school seeking a unique design for its hood. For these purposes he will maintain an up to date file of all the designs of which he is notified.

Faculty Colors

The following colors are associated with the various faculties. It is mandatory that they be used on hoods and optional that they be on the tassels and the velvet used with doctor's gowns. Those marked with an asterisk (*) do not appear on the official list of the 1959 committee of the American Council on Education. They are, however, in current use.

Faculty	Color	Plate Number
1. Agriculture	Maize	III
2. Arts, Letters, Humanities	White	I
3. Commerce, Accountancy, Business	Drab	IV
4. Dentistry	Lilac	XII
5. Economics	Copper	VII
6. Education	Light Blue	V
7. Engineering	Orange	IX
8. Fine Arts, including Architecture	Brown	XI
9. Forestry	Russet	XVII
10. Journalism	Crimson	XIII
11. Law	Purple	II
12. Library Science	Lemon	XXX
13. Medicine	Green	XV
14. Music	Pink	XXIII
15. Nursing	Apricot	XVI
16. *Optometry	Sea Foam Green	X
17. Oratory (Speech)	Silver Gray	XIX
18. Pharmacy	Olive Green	XVIII
19. Philosophy	Dark Blue	XIV
20. Physical Education	Sage Green	XX
21. *Podiatry-Chiropody	Nile Green	XXI
22. Public Administration, including Foreign Service	Peacock Blue	XXII
23. Public Health	Salmon Pink	XXVII
24. Science	Golden Yellow	VIII
25. *Social Science	Cream	XXV
26. Social Work	Citron	XXVI
27. Theology	Scarlet	VI
28. Veterinary Science	Gray	XXVIII

In addition to the foregoing which are in current use, the following colors have at one time been used; Dark Crimson, Humanics; Cerise, Naprapathy; Rose, Philanthropy.

Hood Designs

The following are illustrated on the correspondingly numbered plates.

1. Single Color.

2. Chevron. (Ch.) This is point down.

3. Chevron Reversed. (Ch. Rev.) This is point up.

4. Two Chevrons. (Chs.) The chevrons are separated by the color of the lining.

5. Two Chevrons Reversed. (Chs. Rev.)

6. Three Chevrons.

7. Three Chevrons Reversed.

8. Double Chevron. The two parts of the chevron are not separated by the color of the lining.

9. Double Chevron Reversed.

10. Triple Chevron.

11. Triple Chevron Reversed.

12. Party per Chevron. (per Ch.)

13. Party per Chevron Reversed. (per Ch. Rev.)

14. Bar. This might be called a fess in classical heraldry, but for consistency here it is called a bar.

15. Two Bars. The bars are separated by the color of the lining.

16. Three Bars.

17. Double Bar. The bars are not separated.

18. Triple Bar.

19. Per Bar. This is the classical party per fess.

20. Pale.

21. Two Pales. This is the classical two pallets.

22. Double Pale.

23. Party per Pale.

24. Cross.

25. Per Cross. This is also known as Quarterly in classical heraldry. If only two colors are used in a description the first mentioned is in the upper left and

lower right and the second is in the upper right and lower left. If more than two are used they are given in the order of upper left, upper right, lower left, lower right.

26. Saltire. (Slt.)

27. Per Saltire. (Per Slt.) If only two colors are used in a description the first mentioned is at the top and bottom and the second is at the sides. If more than two are used they are given in the order of top, right, bottom, left.

28. Checky. (Chky.) There is no need to specify which color goes where.

29. Lozengy. (Lgy.) There is no need to specify which color goes where.

30. Tartan. If the tartan is well known there is no need to go beyond naming it. If description is needed the Logan system may be employed. This is based on relative proportions using one-eighth inch in the full sized cloth as a unit. It is illustrated in the section of this book dealing with Tartan Hoods. Since real, as contrasted to currently designed, tartans pertain to clans, septs, regiments, districts or the clergy it is obvious that there should be some connection with, or permission from, the using group before an American college adopts an existing design.

99. This is for all code hoods whose linings do not fit any of the foregoing patterns. As a particular design becomes popular enough to warrant a number one may be assigned.

100. All non-code hoods used by American institutions.

Note: Occasionally a hood will be found which fits into two of these categories. St. Norbert College for example is Per Pale, White and Green, a Yellow Chevron overall. Its pattern is 23-2 or, with colors, 23bh-2c.

Hood Lining Colors

a. Black	f. Orange
b. White and Silver	g. Purple
c. Yellow and Gold	h. Green
d. Red	i. Brown
e. Blue	j. Gray

Every hood lining color is placed into one of these categories. Thus cerise is in d. as a red and mauve is in g. as a purple. The classification of a hood which was Cerise, Two Mauve Chs. Rev. would be 5dg. It would be found with Cardinal, Two Orchid Chs. Rev., Pink, Two Lavender Chs. Rev. and others of that extremely unlikely combination.

Hoods—Institutions

Abilene Christian C, Tex., 1906	Purple, White Ch.
Adams St. C, Colo., 1921	Kelly Green, White Ch.
Adelphi C, N. Y., 1896	Gold, Brown Ch.
Adrian C, Mich., 1859	Gold, Black Ch.
Agnes Scott C, Ga., 1889	Purple, White Ch.
Akron, U of, Ohio, 1870	Navy Blue, Old Gold Ch.
Alabama C, Ala., 1896	Purple, Gold Ch. Rev.
Alabama, U of, Ala., 1831	Crimson, White Ch.
Alaska, U of, Alaska, 1915	Gold, Royal Blue Ch.
Albany, C of Ed at, N. Y. (SUNY) 1844	Purple, Gold Ch.
Albertus Magnus C, Conn., 1925	White, Yale Blue Ch.
Albion C, Mich., 1835	Royal Purple, Two Lemon Gold Chs.
Albright C, Pa., 1856	Cardinal, White Ch. Rev.
Alderson-Broadus C, W. Va., 1871	Gold, Blue Ch.
Alfred U, N. Y., 1857	Purple, Two Old Gold Chs.
Allegheny C, Pa., 1815	Blue, Old Gold Ch.
Allen U, S. C., 1870	Blue, Gold Ch.
Alliance C, Pa., 1912	Red, White Ch.
Alma C, Mich., 1886	Maroon, Cream Ch. Rev.
Alverno C, Wis., 1936	Old Gold, Brown Ch.
American Conservatory, Ill., 1886	Light Blue charged with Gold Circle
American International C, Mass., 1885	Per Ch., Old Gold, White
American U, D. C., 1893	Red, White Ch., Blue
American U of Beirut, Lebanon, 1863	Scarlet, Two White Chs.
Amherst C, Mass., 1821	Purple, White Ch.
Anderson C, Ind., 1917	Orange, Black Ch.
Andover Newton Theo Sch	see Andover Theo Sch and Newton Theological Institution
Andover Theo Sem, Mass., 1807	Electric Blue
Andrews U, Mich., 1874	Unofficial Bachelor, Green, White Ch.
Official for graduate degrees	Gold, Two Black Chs.
Anna Maria C for Women, Mass., 1946	Royal Blue, White Ch.
Annhurst C, Conn., 1941	Purple, White Ch.
Antioch C, Ohio, 1852	No Hood
Appalachian St Tchers C, N. C., 1903	Black, Gold, Ch.
Aquinas C, Mich., 1922	Maroon, Silver Gray Ch. Rev.
Arizona St C, Ariz., 1899	Gold, Royal Blue Ch.
Arizona St U, Ariz., 1885	Maroon, Gold Ch.

Arizona, U of, Ariz., 1885	National Red, Blue Ch.
Arkansas A, M, and Normal C, Ark., 1873	No Hood
Arkansas A and M C, Ark., 1909	Green, White Ch.
Arkansas C, Ark., 1872	No Hood
Arkansas Polytechnic C, Ark., 1909	No Hood
Arkansas St C, Ark., 1909	Red, Black Ch.
Arkansas St Tchers C, Ark., 1907	Royal Purple, Silver Gray Ch., Education Blue
Arkansas, U of, Ark., 1871	Cardinal, White Ch.
Armstrong C, Calif., 1918	Carmine, Ultramarine Ch.
Aroostock St Tchers C, Maine, 1903	Royal Blue, Gold Ch.
Art Inst of Chicago, Ill., 1863	See section on non-code hoods
Asbury C, Ky., 1890	Purple, White Ch.
Assumption C, Mass., 1904	Per Ch., White, Dark Blue
Atlanta U, Ga., 1865	Crimson, Gray Ch.
Atlantic Christian C, N. C., 1902	Royal Blue, White Ch.
Auburn U, Ala., 1856	Burnt Orange, Royal Blue Ch.
Augustana C, S. Dak., 1860	Per Ch., Old Gold, Royal Blue
Augustana Theo Sem., Ill., 1860	Blue, Gold Ch.
Aurora C, Ill., 1893	Royal Blue, White Ch.
Austin C, Texas, 1849	Crimson, Gold Ch.
Austin Peay St C, Tenn., 1927	Scarlet, White Ch.
Austin Presbyterian Theo Sem, Tex., 1902	Per Ch., White, Royal Blue
Azusa C, Calif., 1899	Royal Blue, White Ch.
Baker U, Kans., 1858	Cadmium Orange
Baldwin-Wallace C, Ohio, 1845	Brown, Gold Ch.
Ball St Tchers C, Ind., 1918	Red, White Ch.
Baltimore, U of, Md., 1925	Maroon, White Ch.
Bangor Theo Sem, Maine, 1814	Navy Blue, Crimson Ch.
Baptist Bible Sem, N. Y., 1932	Unofficial, Royal Blue, White Ch.
Bard C, N. Y., 1860	Scarlet, White Ch.
Barrington C, R. I., 1950	Purple, Bright Gold Ch.
Barry C, Fla., 1940	Silver Gray, Black Ch., Red
Bates C, Maine, 1864	Garnet
Baylor U, Tex., 1845	Green, Gold Ch.
Beaver C, Pa., 1853	Scarlet, Gray Ch.
Bellarmine C, Ky., 1950	Crimson, Pearl Gray Ch.
Belmont Abbey C, N. C., 1876	Crimson, White Ch.
Beloit C, Wis., 1846	Dark Gold
Bemidji St C, Minn., 1913	Per Ch, Kelly Green, White
Benedictine Heights C, Okla., 1916	Royal Blue, Gold Ch.
Bennington C, Vt., 1925	Royal Midnight Blue
Berea C, Ky., 1855	Yale Blue, White Ch.
Berkeley Baptist Divinity Sch, Calif., 1871	Purple, Gold Ch.
Berkeley Divinity Sch, Conn., 1854	See section on non-code hoods

Berkshire Christian C, Mass., 1897 . . . . . Purple, White Bar
Berry C, Ga., 1902 . . . . Blue, Silver Ch.
Bethany Bible C, Calif., 1919 . . Robin's Egg Blue, Two White Chs, Rev.
Bethany Biblical Sem, Ill., 1905 . . . . . Navy Blue, White Ch.
Bethany C, Kans., 1881 . . . . . Per Ch., Lemon, Royal Blue
Bethany C, W. Va., 1840 . . . . . . Green, White Ch.
Bethel C, Tenn., 1923 . . . . . Purple, Gold Ch., Rev.
Bethel C and Sem, Minn., 1871 . . . . Gold, Royal Blue Ch.
Bethune-Cookman C, Fla., 1904 . . . . . Maroon, Gold Ch.
Bible, C of, Ky., 1865 . . . . . . Crimson, White Ch.
Biblical Sem in New York, N. Y., 1900 . . . . Purple, White Ch.
Birmingham-Southern C, Ala., 1856 . . . . Old Gold, Black Ch.
Black Hills Tchers C, S. Dak., 1883 . . . . Purple, Gold Ch.
Blackburn C, Ill., 1857 . . . . . . Old Rose, Black Ch.
Bloomfield C and Sem, N. J., 1868 . . Medium Maroon, Bright Gold Ch.
Bloomsburg St C, Pa., 1839 . . . . . Maroon, Gold Ch.
Blue Mountain C, Miss., 1873 . . . . . Blue, Gold Ch.
Bluffton C, Ohio, 1913 . . . . . . Purple, White Ch.
Bob Jones U, S. C., 1927 . . . . Royal Blue, White Ch.
Boston C, Mass., 1863 . . . . . . Maroon, Gold Ch.
Boston Cons. of Music, Mass. 1867 . B. Mus, M. Mus. Pink, B.F.A. Saffron
Boston St C, Mass., 1852 . . . . Medium Green, Yellow Ch.
Boston U, Mass., 1839 . . . . . . Scarlet, White Ch.
Bowdoin C, Maine, 1794 . . . . White
Bowling Green C of Commerce, Ky., 1922 . . . . No Hood
Bowling Green St U, Ohio, 1910 . . . Burnt Orange, Brown Ch.
Bradley U, Ill., 1896 . . . . . . Red, White Ch.
Brandeis U, Mass., 1948 . . . . . Wedgewood Blue
Brenau C, Ga., 1878 . . . . . Per Ch., Old Gold, Black
Briar Cliff C, Iowa, 1930 . . . Old Gold, Two Royal Blue Chs.
Bridgeport, U of, Conn., 1927 . . . . . Purple, White Ch.
Bridgewater St C, Mass., 1840 . . . . . . Crimson
Brigham Young U, Utah, 1875 . . . . Per Ch., White, Blue
Brockport, C of Ed at, N. Y., (SUNY) 1841 . . Emerald Green, Gold Ch.
Brooklyn Polytechnic Inst . . . See Polytechnic Inst. of Brooklyn
Brown U, R. I., 1764 . . . . . Seal Brown, Cardinal Ch.
Bryn Mawr C, Pa., 1885 . . . . . Old Gold, White Ch.
Bucknell U, Pa., 1846 . . . . . Orange, Yale Blue Ch.
Buena Vista College, Iowa 1891 . . . . Dark Blue, Gold Ch.
Buffalo, C of Ed at, N. Y., (SUNY) 1867 . . Dark Blue, Gold Ch.
Buffalo, U of, N. Y., 1846 . . . . Yale Blue, White Ch.
Butler U, Ind., 1855 . . . . . Royal Blue, White Ch.
Cabrini C, Pa., 1957 . . . . . Scarlet, Old Gold Ch.
California Baptist Theo Sem, Calif., 1944 . . . Royal Blue, Gold Ch.

California Inst of Technology, Calif., 1891 . . . . Orange, White Ch.
California Podiatry C, Calif., 1914 . . . . . . Gold
California St Polytechnic C, Calif., 1901 . Kelly Green, Two Yellow Gold Chs.
California U of Calif., 1868 . . . . . Gold, Yale Blue Ch.
Calvin C, Mich., 1876 . . . . Maroon, Gold Ch.
Campbellsville C, Ky., 1906 . . . . . . No Hood
Canasius C, N. Y., 1870 . . . . . Royal Blue, Gold Ch.
Capital U, Ohio, 1850 . . . Medium Purple, Two White Chs.
Cardinal Cushing C, Mass., 1952 . . . . Cardinal, White Ch.
Carleton C, Minn., 1866 . . . . Maize, Royal Blue Ch.
Carnegie Inst of Technology, Pa., 1900 . . . . Carnegie Tartan
Carroll C, Mont., 1909 . . . . Royal Purple, Old Gold Ch.
Carroll C, Wis., 1846 . . . . . . White, Orange Ch.
Carson-Newman C, Tenn., 1851 . . . . . No Hood
Carthage C, Ill., 1847 . . . . . . Crimson, White Ch.
Carver Sch of Missions and Social Work, Ky., 1907 . . Purple, Gold Ch.
Cascade C, Oregon, 1918 . . . . . Crimson, White Ch.
Case Inst of Technology, Ohio, 1880 . . . Per Ch., Brown, White
Castleton Teachers C, Vt., 1867 . . . . . No Hood
Catawba C, N. C., 1851 . . . . . Yale Blue, White Ch.
Cathedral C of the Immaculate Conception, N. Y., 1914 . . Light Blue
Catholic U of America, D. C., 1887 . . . . Gold, White Ch.

(This is from the University, observation indicates that graduates are actually
wearing Gold, White Bar.)

Catholic U of Puerto Rico, Puerto Rico, 1948 . . Light Blue, White Ch.
Cedar Crest C, Pa., 1867 . . . . Golden Yellow, White Ch.
Central Baptist Sem, Kans., 1901 . . . Scarlet, Two Old Gold Chs.
Central Bible Inst and Sem, Mo., 1922 . . . Royal Blue, White Ch.
Central C, Iowa, 1853 . . . . . . Scarlet, White Ch.
Central C, Mo., 1871 . . . . Nile Green, Black Ch.
*Central High School of Phila., 1836 . . . Crimson, Gold Ch.

* Degree Granting by act of Pennsylvania legislature. No longer college level
but graduates receive the B.A. or B.S. degree and may wear the bachelor's hood lined
as described.

Central Connecticut St C, Conn., 1849 . . . Royal Blue, White Ch.
Central Michigan U, Mich., 1892 . . . . Maroon, Gold Ch.
Central Missouri St C, Mo., 1871 . . . . . Red, Black Ch.
Central St C, Ohio, 1887 . . . . . Scarlet, Gold Ch., Rev.
Central Wesleyan C, S. C., 1909 . . . Medium Blue, Gold Ch.
Centre C of Kentucky, Ky., 1819 . . . . White, Gold Ch.
Chadron St Tchers C, Nebr., 1911 . . Dark Cardinal, White Ch. Rev.
Chaminade C of Honolulu, Hawaii, 1955 . . . Royal Blue, White Ch.
Chapman C, Calif., 1861 . Cardinal, small gray ch., on each side, hidden when worn
Charleston, C of, S. C., 1770 . . . . . . No Hood

Chattanooga, U of, Tenn., 1886 . . . Earned, Old Gold, Royal Blue Ch.
Honorary, Per Ch., Old Gold, Royal Blue
Chatham C, Penn., 1869 . . . . . Medium Purple, White Ch.
Chestnut Hill C of Sisters of St. Joseph, Penn., 1871 . Per Ch., Gold, Brown
Cheney St C, Penn., 1837 . . . . . Royal Blue, White Ch.
Chicago Art Inst . . . . . . See Art Inst of Chicago
Chicago C of Chiropody, Ill., 1931 . . . . Purple, Gold Ch.
Chicago C of Osteopathy, Ill., 1913 . . . Seafoam Green
Chicago Conservatory C, Ill., 1857 . . . Gold, Two Purple Chs.
Chicago-Kent C of Law, Ill., 1888 . . . . Royal Blue, Old Gold Ch.
Chicago Lutheran Theo Sem, Ill., 1891 . . Per Ch., Old Gold, Olive Green
Chicago Medical Sch, Ill., 1912 . . . . Purple, Gold Ch.
Chicago Tchers C, Ill., 1869 . . . . Dark Green, White Ch.
Chicago, U of, Ill., 1890 . . . . Maroon
Chico St C, Calif., 1887 . . . . . . Cardinal, White Ch.
Chouinard Art Inst, Calif., 1921 . . . . Burnt Orange
Christian Brothers C, Tenn., 1854 . . . . White, Scarlet Ch.
Christian Theo Sem, Ind., 1924 . . . . Silver Gray, Scarlet Ch.
Church Divinity Sch of the Pacific, Calif. . See section on non-code hoods
Cincinnati Bible Sem, Ohio, 1924 . . . . Purple, Gold Ch.
Cincinnati College-Conservatory of Music, Ohio, 1867 Pearl Gray, Light Blue Ch.
Cincinnati, U of, Ohio, 1819 . . . Bright Red, Two Black Chs.
Citadel, The, S. C., 1842 . . . . . Light Blue, White Ch.
City College of New York, N. Y., 1847 . . . . Lavender
Claremont Men's C, Calif., 1946 . . . . Maroon, White Ch.
Clark U, Mass., 1887 . . . . . White, Emerald Green Ch.
Cleary C, Mich., 1883 . . . . . Navy Blue, Scarlet Ch. Rev.
Clarke C, Iowa, 1843 . . White, Two Chs., Upper Purple, Lower Gold
Clemson C, S. C., 1889 . . . Northwestern Purple, Burnt Orange Ch.
Cleveland-Marshall Law Sch, Ohio, 1897 . . . Brown, Gold Ch.
Coe C, Iowa, 1851 . . . . . Per Ch., Gold, Crimson
Coker C, S. C., 1908 . . . . No Hood
Colby C, Maine, 1813 . . . . . Per Ch., Yale Blue, Gray
Colgate-Rochester Divinity Sch, N. Y., 1817 . . . Yellow, Maroon Ch.
College-Conservatory of Music of Cincinnati . . See under Cincinnati
College Misericordia . . . . . See Misericordia, College
Colorado C, Colo., 1874 . . . . . . Black, Gold Ch.
Colorado Sch of Mines, Colo., 1874 . . Per Ch., Light Navy, Silver Gray
Colorado St C, Colo., 1889 . . . . . Old Gold, Purple Ch.
Colorado State U, Colo., 1870 . . Pumpkin Yellow, Alfalfa Green Ch.
Colorado, U of, Colo., 1876 . . . . . Gold, Silver Gray Ch.
Columbia Theo Sem, Ga., 1828 . . . . Blue, Old Gold Ch.
Columbia U, N. Y., 1754 . . . . . Light Blue, White Ch.
Concord C, W. Va., 1875 . . . . . . Maroon, Gray Ch.

Concordia C, Minn., 1891	No Hood
Concordia Sem, Mo., 1839	Myrtle Green, Yellow Gold Ch.
Concordia Tchers C, Ill., 1864	Maroon, Gold Ch.
Concordia Tchers C, Nebr., 1894	Royal Blue, White Ch.
Concordia Theo Sem, Ill., 1846	Royal Blue, White Ch.
Connecticut C, Conn., 1911	Blue
Connecticut, U of, Conn., 1881	National Flag Blue, White Ch.
Conservative Baptist Theo Sem, Colo., 1950	Scarlet, Silver Ch.
Converse C, S. C., 1889	Gold, Purple Ch.
Cooper Union, N. Y., 1859	Maroon, Gold Ch.
Cornell C, Iowa, 1853	Purple, Three White Chs.
Cornell U, N. Y., 1865	Carnelian (Red), Two White Chs.
Cortland, C of Ed at, N. Y. (SUNY) 1863	Per Ch., White, Scarlet
Covenant C and Covenant Theo Sem, Mo., 1955	Clergy Tartan
Cranbrook Academy of Art, N. J., 1942	White, Three Red Chs. Rev. (varying widths)
Creighton U, Nebr., 1878	Per Ch., Light Blue, White
Crozer Theo Sem, Penn., 1867	Blue, White Ch.
Culver-Stockton C, Mo., 1853	White, Royal Blue Ch.
Curtis Inst of Music, Penn., 1924	Scarlet, White Ch.
Dakota Wesleyan U, S. Dak., 1885	Royal Blue, White Ch.
Dallas Theo Sem, Tex., 1924	Purple, Yellow Ch.
Dallas, U of, Tex., 1955	Navy Blue, White Ch.
Dana C, Nebr., 1884	Red, White Ch.
Danbury St C, Conn., 1903	Yale or Connecticut Blue
Dartmouth C, N. H., 1769	Dark Green
David Lipscomb C, Tenn., 1891	Purple, Gold Ch.
Davidson C, N. C., 1837	Red
Dayton, U of, Ohio, 1850	Red, Light Blue Ch.
Delaware, U of, Del., 1833	Blue, Golden Yellow Ch.
De Paul U, Ill., 1898	Blue, Red Ch.
De Pauw U, Ind., 1837	Old Gold
Delta St C, Miss., 1924	No Hood
Denison U, Ohio, 1831	Red, White Ch.
Denver, U of, Colo., 1864	Crimson, Gold Ch.
Detroit C of Law, Mich., 1891	Red, White Ch.
Detroit Inst of Musical Art, Mich., 1914	Per Pale, Blue, Gold
Detroit, U of, Mich., 1877	Per Ch., Cardinal, White
Dickinson C, Penn., 1773	Scarlet, White Ch.
Dickinson Sch of Law, Penn., 1834	Red, White Ch.
Divinity Sch in Philadelphia, Penn., 1856	White charged with an equal armed red cross
Doane C, Nebr., 1872	Gold, Black Ch.
Dominican C, Wis., 1946	White, Black Ch.

Dominican C of San Rafael, Calif., 1890 . . . . Gold, White Ch.
Drake U, Iowa, 1881 . . . . Royal Blue, White Ch.
Drew U, N. J., 1867 . . . Bachelor of Arts...Lincoln Green, Gold Ch.
                               Other degrees...Oxford Blue, Lincoln Green Ch.
Drexel Inst of Technology, Penn., 1891 . . . . . Old Gold
Dropsie C, Penn., 1907 . . . . . . Yale Blue, Gold Ch.
Drury C, Mo., 1873 . . . . . . Gray, Two Scarlet Chs.
Dunbarton C of the Holy Cross, D. C., 1935 . . . Royal Blue, Gold Ch.
Dubuque, U of, Iowa, 1852 . . . . . White, Yale Blue Ch.
Duchesne C of the Sacred Heart, Nebr., 1915 . Hunter Green, Bright Gold Ch.
Duke U, N. C., 1838 . . . . . . Yale Blue, White Ch.
Duquesne U, Penn., 1878 . . . Gules (Red), Pale Azure Ch. Rev.
Dyke C, Ohio, 1848 . . . . . White, Two Royal Blue Chs.
D'Youvile C, N. Y., 1908 . . . . . . White, Red Ch.
Earlham C, Ind., 1847 . . . . . . Maroon, White Ch.
East Carolina C, N. C., 1907 . . . . . Purple, Gold Ch.
East Central St C, Okla., 1909 . . . Burnt Orange, Black Ch. Rev.
East Stroudsburg St C, Penn., 1893 . . . . Red, Black Ch.
East Tennessee St C, Tenn., 1911 . . . . Royal Blue, Gold Ch.
East Texas Baptist C, Tex., 1912 . . . Royal Blue, Old Gold Ch.
East Texas State College, Tex., 1889 . . . . Blue, Gold Ch.
Eastern Baptist Theo Sem, Pa., 1925 . . . . Royal Blue, White Ch.
Eastern Illinois U, Ill., 1895 . . Medium Blue, Two Silver Gray Chs. Rev.
Eastern Kentucky St C, Ky., 1906 . . . . White, Maroon Ch.
Eastern Michigan U, Mich., 1849 . . . . Green, White Ch.
Eastern Mennonite C, Pa., 1917 . . . . . No Hood
Eastern Montana C of Ed, Mont., 1927 . . . . . Old Gold
Eastern Nazarene C, Mass., 1900 . . . . . Red, White Ch.
Eastern New Mexico U, New Mexico, 1934 . . . . Green, Silver Ch.
Eastern Oregon C, Oreg., 1929 . . . . Royal Blue, Gold Ch.
Eastern Pilgrim C, Pa., 1921 . . . . Royal Blue, White Ch.
Eastern Washington St C, Wash., 1890 . . . . Red, White Ch.
Eau Claire St C, Wis., 1916 . . . . Old Gold, Blue Ch.
Edinboro St C, Pa., 1857 . . . . . Red, White Ch.
Elizabethtown C, Pa., 1899 . . . . . Blue, Gray Ch.
Ellendale St Tchers C, N. Dak., 1889 . . . . . No Hood
Elmhurst C, Ill., 1871 . . . . . . Blue, White Ch.
Elmira C, N. Y., 1855 . . . . . . Per Ch., Gold, Purple
Elon College, N. C., 1889 . . . . . Maroon, Gold Ch.
Emmanuel C, Mass., 1919 . . . . . Per Ch., Blue, Gold
Emmanuel Missionary C, Mich. . . . . . See Andrews U.
Emerson C, Mass., 1880 . . . . . Per Bar, Purple, Gold
Emory University, Ga., 1836 . . . . . Blue, Gold Ch.
Eureka C, Ill., 1855 . . . . No Hood

Evangel C, Mo., 1955 . . . . No Hood
Evangelical Congregational Sch of Theology, Pa., 1953 . . Yellow, Red Ch.
Evangelical Theo Sem, Ill., 1873 . . . . . Purple, 4″ White Ch.
Fairfield U, Conn., 1942 . . . . Cardinal
Fairmont St C, W. Va., 1865 . . . . No Hood
Fairleigh Dickinson U, N. J., 1941 . . . . . Maroon, White Ch.
Faith Theo Sem, Penn., 1937 . . . . . Crimson, Gold Ch. Rev.
Farmington St Tchers C, Maine, 1864 . . . . Red, White Ch.
Fayetteville St Tchers C, N. C., 1877 . . . . Royal Blue, White Ch.
Fenn C, Ohio, 1923 . . . . Crimson, Gray Ch.
Ferris Inst, Mich., 1884 . . . . . . Crimson, Gold Ch.
Findlay C, Ohio, 1882 . . . . . . Orange, Black Ch.
Florence St C, Ala., 1830 . . . . . . Purple, Gold Ch.
Florida A and M U, Fla., 1887 . . . . . Orange, Green Ch.
Florida Southern C, Fla., 1885 . . . . . . Blood Red
Florida St U, Fla., 1857 . . . . . . Garnet, Gold Ch.
Florida, U of, Fla., 1853 . . . . . . Orange, Blue Ch.
Fontbonne C, Mo., 1917 . . . . . . Gold, Purple Ch.
Fordham U, N. Y., 1841 . . . . Maroon
Fort Hays Kansas St C, Kans., 1902 . . . . . . Old Gold
Franklin and Marshall C, Penn., 1787 . . . Yale Blue, White Ch.
Franklin C of Indiana, Ind., 1834 . . . Navy Blue, Old Gold Ch.
Franklin U, Ohio, 1902 . . . . . Royal Blue, White Ch.
Fredonia, St C of Ed at, N. Y. (SUNY) 1867 . . Yale Blue, Gold Ch.
Free Will Baptist Bible C, Tenn., 1942 . . . Blue, White Ch. Rev.
Fresno St C, Calif., 1911 . . . . Cardinal, Royal Blue Ch.
Friends U, Kans., 1898 . . . . No Hood
Frostburg St Tchers C, Md., 1898 . . . . Black, Yellow Ch.
Fuller Theo Sem, Calif., 1947 . . . Royal Blue, Three Gold Chs.
Furman U, S. C., 1826 . . . . No Hood
Gannon C, Penn., 1944 . . . . . . Maroon, Gold Ch.
General Theo Sem, N. Y., 1817 . . . See section on non-code hoods
Geneseo, C of Ed at, N. Y., (SUNY) 1867 . . Royal Blue, Gold Yellow Ch.
Geneva C, Penn., 1848 . . . . . Old Gold, White Ch.
George Fox C, Oreg., 1891 . . . . Navy Blue, Old Gold Ch.
George Peabody C for Tchers, Tenn., 1875 . . . M.A. and Ph.D.,
   Garnet, Turquoise Ch. Rev.;
   Ed.S. (Specialist in Education) Turquoise, Garnet Ch. (N.B. Velvet Trim
   is white rather than Ed.'s light blue); Ed.D., Garnet, Turquoise Ch.
George Washington U, D. C., 1821 . . . . Dark Blue, Buff Ch.
George Williams C, Ill., 1890 . . . . Royal Blue, Antique Gold Ch.
Georgetown C, Ky., 1829 . . . . . . Orange, Black Ch.
Georgetown U, D. C., 1789 . . . Confederate Gray, Union Blue Ch.
Georgia Inst of Tech, Ga., 1888 . . . . Old Gold, White Ch.

Georgia Southern C, Ga., 1908   .   .   .   .   Biarritz Blue, White Ch.
Georgia St C of Bus Ad, Ga., 1914   .   .   Silver Gray, wide Spectrum Red Ch.
Georgia St C for Women, Ga.   .   .   .   See Woman's College of Georgia
Georgia, U of, Ga., 1785   .   .   .   .   .   Per Ch., Bright Red, Black
Gettysburg C, Penn., 1832   .   .   .   .   .   Blue, Orange Ch., Rev.
Glassboro St C, N. J., 1923   .   .   .   .   .   Gold, Brown Ch.
Goddard C, Vt., 1938   .   .   .   .   No Hood
Golden Gate Baptist Theo Sem, Calif., 1948   .   .   Gold, Purple Ch.
Golden Gate C, Calif., 1901   .   .   .   .   .   Maroon, Gold Ch.
Gonzaga U, Wash., 1887   .   .   .   .   .   .   Blue, White Ch.
Good Cousel C, N. Y., 1923   .   .   .   .   .   Crimson, Gold Ch.
Gordon Divinity Sch, Mass., 1889   .   .   .   .   .   .   Yale Blue
Gorham St C for Tchers, Maine, 1938   .   .   .   Forest Green, White Ch.
Goucher C, Md., 1885   .   .   .   .   Blue, Gold Ch.
Grace C, Ind., 1937   .   .   .   .   .   .   Yellow Gold, White Ch.
Graceland C, Iowa, 1895   .   .   .   .   .   Old Gold, Blue Ch.
Grand Canyon C, Ariz., 1949   .   .   .   .   .   Purple, White Ch.
Grand Rapids Baptist Theo Sem and Bible Inst, Mich., 1945 . Royal Blue, Gold Ch.
Great Falls, C of, Mont., 1932   .   .   .   .   Azure Blue, Gold Ch.
Greenville C, Ill., 1892   .   .   .   .   .   .   Black, Orange Ch.
Guilford C, N. C., 1937   .   .   .   .   .   Gray, Two Crimson Chs.
Gustavus Adolphus C, Minn., 1862   .   .   .   Bright Gold, Black Ch.
Hahnemann Medical C, Penn., 1848   .   .   .   .   Blue, Gold Ch.
Hamilton C, N. Y., 1812   .   .   Continental Blue, Continental Buff Ch.
Hamline U, Minn., 1854   .   .   .   .   .   .   Gray, Red Ch.
Hampton Inst, Va., 1868   .   .   .   .   Royal Blue, White Ch. Rev.
Hanover C, Ind., 1827   .   .   .   .   .   Crimson, Navy Blue Ch.
Hardin Simmons U, Tex., 1891   .   .   .   .   Purple, Gold Ch. Rev.
Harding C, Ark., 1924   .   .   .   .   .   .   Black, Old Gold Ch.
Harpur C, N. Y. (SUNY) 1948   .   .   .   .   Navy Blue, Gold Ch.
Harris Tchers C, Mo., 1857   .   .   .   .   .   Gold, Black Ch.
Hartford, U of, Conn., 1956   .   .   .   .   .   Scarlet, White Ch.
Hartwick C, N. Y., 1928   .   .   .   .   .   Royal Blue, White Ch.
Harvard U, Mass., 1636   ..   .   .   .   See section on non-code hoods
Harvey Mudd C, Calif., 1955   .   .   .   .   .   .   No Hood
Hastings C, Nebr., 1882   .   .   .   .   .   Maroon, Two White Chs.
Haverford C, Penn., 1833   .   .   .   .   .   .   Red, Black Ch.
Hawaii, U of, Hawaii, 1907   .   .   .   Emerald Green, Two White Chs.
Hebrew Union C, Ohio, 1875   .   .   .   .   .   .   Old Gold
Heidelberg C, Ohio, 1850   .   .   Red, Three Chs., Black, Orange, Black
Henderson St Tchers C, Ark., 1929   .   .   .   Rainwine, Silver Gray Ch.
Hendrix C, Ark., 1884   .   .   .   .   .   .   Orange, Black Ch.
High Point C, N. C., 1924   .   .   .   .   .   .   Purple, White Ch.
Hillsdale C, Mich., 1844   .   .   .   .   .   Royal Blue, White Ch.

Hiram C, Ohio, 1850	Cherry Red, Sky Blue Ch.
Hobart C, N. Y., 1822	Per Ch., Orange, Purple
Hofstra C, N. Y., 1935	Royal Blue, Gold Ch.
Hollins C, Va., 1842	Piper Green, Gold Ch., Bright Green
Holy Cross, C of the, Mass., 1843	Royal Purple
Holy Family C, Wis., 1935	Virgin Blue, White Ch.
Holy Names C, Wash., 1889	Purple, Gold Ch.
Holy Names, C of the, Calif., 1880	Crimson, White Ch.
Holy Trinity Orthodox Sem, N. Y., 1948	White, Blue Ch., Red
Hood C, Md., 1893	Navy Blue, Silver Gray Ch.
Hope C, Mich., 1851	Per Ch. Orange, Blue
Houghton C, N. Y., 1883	Gold, Purple Ch.
Houston, U of, Tex., 1934	Red, White Ch., Rev.
Howard C, Ala., 1842	Crimson, Royal Blue Ch.
Howard Payne C, Tex., 1889	Navy Blue, Old Gold Ch.
Howard U, D. C., 1867	Royal Blue, White Ch.
Humboldt St C, Calif., 1913	Kelly Green, Yellow Gold Ch.
Hunter C, N. Y., 1870	Lavender, White Ch.
Huntington C, Ind., 1897	Apple Green, Scarlet Ch.
Idaho, C of, Idaho, 1891	Purple, Gold Ch.
Idaho St C, Idaho, 1901	Orange, Black Ch.
Idaho, U of, Idaho, 1889	Honorary Degrees, Silver, Gold Bar
	Projected for Earned Degrees, Silver, Two Gold Chs.
Iliff Sch of Theology, Colo., 1892	Light Blue, White Ch.
Illinois C, Ill., 1829	Yale Blue, Three White Chs.
Illinois C of Optometry, Ill., 1872	Royal Blue, Triple Ch., White, Seafoam Green, White
Illinois Inst of Tech., Ill., 1892	Scarlet, Silver Gray Ch.
Illinois St Normal U, Ill., 1857	Scarlet, White Ch.
Illinois, U of, Ill., 1868	Navy Blue, Two Orange Chs.
Illinois Wesleyan U, Ill., 1850	Per Ch., Green—White
Immaculata C, Penn., 1920	Columbia Blue, White Ch.
Immaculate Heart C, Calif., 1916	Purple, White Ch.
Indiana Central C, Ind., 1902	Cardinal, Gray Ch.
Indiana St C, Penn., 1871	Maroon, Slate Ch.
Indiana St C, Ind., 1865	Blue, White Ch.
Indiana U, Ind., 1820	Crimson, Cream Ch.
Iowa St U, Iowa, 1858	Per Ch., Old Gold, Cardinal
Iowa, St U of, Iowa, 1847	Old Gold
Iowa Wesleyan C, 1842	White, Purple Bar
Ithaca C, N. Y., 1892	Dark Blue, Gold Ch.
Jamestown C, N. Dak., 1884	Orange, Black Ch.
Jarvis Christian C, Tex., 1912	Gold, Three Blue Chs.
Jefferson Medical C of Phila, Penn., 1824	Black, Baby Blue Ch.

Jersey City St C, N. J., 1946   .   .   .   .   .   Green, Gold Ch.
Jewish Studies, C of, Ill., 1925   .   .   .   Light Blue, White Ch. Rev.
Jewish Theo Sem of America, N. Y., 1902   .   .   .   Light Blue, White Ch.
John Brown U, Ark., 1917   .   .   .   .   Royal Blue, Old Gold Ch.
John Carroll U, Ohio, 1886   .   .   .   .   Navy Blue, Yellow Gold Ch.
John Herron Art Sch, Ind., 1902   .   .   .   .   Gold, Royal Blue Ch.
Johns Hopkins U, Md., 1876   .   .   .   .   .   Black, Old Gold Ch.
Johnson C. Smith U, N. C., 1867   .   .   .   Gold, Admiral Blue Ch.
Johnson Tchers C, Vt., 1827   .   .   .   .   Dark Green, White Ch.
Judson C, Ala., 1838   .   .   .   .   Red, Black Ch.
Julliard Sch of Music, N. Y., 1906   .   .   .   .   Scarlet, Royal Blue Ch.
Juniata C, Penn., 1876   .   .   .   .   .   Yale Blue, Old Gold Ch.
Kalamazoo C, Mich., 1833   .   .   .   .   Orange, Three Black Chs.
Kansas City Bible C, Mo., 1932   .   .   .   Red, Double Ch., White-Gold
Kansas City C of Osteopathy and Surgery, Mo., 1916   .   .   Purple, Gold Ch.
Kansas City, U of, Mo., 1929   .   .   .   .   Royal Blue, Gold Ch.
Kansas St C of Pittsburg, Kans., 1903   .   .   .   Yellow Gold, Crimson Ch.
Kansas St U, Kans., 1863   .   .   .   .   .   Purple, Two White Chs.
Kansas, U of, Kans., 1865   .   .   .   .   Harvard Crimson, Yale Blue Ch.
Kansas Wesleyan U, Kans., 1886   .   .   .   .   Purple, Gold Ch. Rev.
Kearney St Tchers C, Nebr., 1905   .   .   .   Old Gold, Royal Blue Ch.
Keene Tchers C, N. H., 1909   .   .   .   .   Cardinal, White Ch.
Kentucky, U of, Ky., 1865   .   .   .   .   .   Blue, White Ch.
Kentucky Wesleyan C, Ky., 1858   .   .   .   .   Purple, White Ch.
Kenyon College, Ohio, 1824   .   .   .   .   Mauve
Keuka C, N. Y., 1892   .   .   .   .   .   .   Green, Gold Ch.
King C, Tenn., 1866   .   .   .   .   .   .   Maroon, Blue Ch.
King's C, Penn., 1946   .   .   .   .   .   .   Red, Gold Ch.
Kirksville C of Osteopathy and Surgery, Mo., 1892   .   .   Bright Red
Knox C, Ill., 1837   .   .   .   .   .   .   Purple, Old Gold Ch.
Kutztown St C, Penn., 1866   .   .   .   .   Maroon, Gold Ch.
La Crosse St C, Wis., 1909   .   .   .   .   .   .   Maroon
La Grange C, Ga., 1831   .   .   .   .   .   .   Red, Black Ch.
La Salle C, Penn., 1863   .   .   .   .   .   Old Gold, Navy Blue Ch.
La Sierra C, Calif., 1922   .   .   .   .   .   .   No Hood
La Verne C, Calif., 1908   .   .   Emerald Green, Gold Orange Ch. Rev.
Ladycliff C, N. Y., 1933   .   .   .   .   .   Gold, Three Blue Chs.
Lake Erie C, Ohio, 1856   .   .   .   .   Olive Green, White Ch.
Lake Forest C, Ill., 1857   .   .   .   .   .   Per Ch., Red, Black
Lamar St C of Tech., Tex., 1923   .   .   .   .   Cardinal, White Ch.
Lane C, Tenn., 1878   .   .   .   .   Cardinal, Royal Blue, Ch.
Lancaster Theo Sem, Penn., 1825   .   .   .   .   Scarlet, Gold Ch.
Lander C, S. C., 1872   .   .   .   .   Royal Blue, Daffodil Yellow Ch.
Langston U, Okla., 1897   .   .   .   .   No Hood

Lebanon Valley C, Penn., 1866	Royal Blue, White Ch.
Lemoyne C, Tenn., 1870	Royal Purple, Old Gold Ch.
Lesley C, Mass., 1909	Green, Gold Ch.
Lewi, M. J., College of Podiatry, N. Y., 1912	Turquoise, Gold Ch.
Lewis and Clark C, Oregon, 1867	Per Ch., Black, Princeton Orange
Limestone C, S. C., 1845	Light Gold, Two White Chs.
Lincoln Bible Inst, Ill., 1944	Scarlet, White Ch.
Lincoln Memorial U, Tenn., 1897	Unofficial, Blue, Gray Ch.
Lincoln U, Penn., 1854	Navy Blue, Burnt Orange Ch.
Linfield C, Oregon, 1849	Purple, Cardinal Ch.
Little Rock U, Ark., 1927	No Hood
Livingston St C, Ala., 1835	Light Blue
Lock Haven St Tchers C, Penn., 1870	No Hood
Loma Linda U (formerly C of Medical Evangelists), Calif., 1905	Gold, Purple Ch.
Long Beach St C, Calif., 1949	Gold, Brown Ch.
Long Island U, N. Y., 1926	Bachelor of Arts, White; Bachelor of Science, Gold
Longwood C, Va., 1884	Royal Blue, White Ch.
Loras C, Iowa, 1839	Per Ch., Purple, Gold
Loretto Heights C, Colo., 1918	White, Green Ch.
Los Angeles C of Optometry, Calif., 1904	Gold, Purple Ch.
Los Angeles Cons. of Music, Calif., 1883	Burgundy, Two Gold Chs.
Los Angeles Pacific C, Calif., 1903	No Hood
Los Angeles St C, Calif., 1947	Gold, Black Ch.
Louisiana C, La., 1906	Orange, Navy Blue Ch.
Louisiana Polytechnic Inst, La., 1894	Cardinal, Royal Blue Ch.
Louisiana State U, 1860	Purple, Gold Ch. Rev.
Louisville, U of, Ky., 1798	Cardinal
Louisville Presbyterian Theo Sem, Ky., 1853	Per Ch., White, National Blue
Lowell Technological Inst, Mass., 1895	Red, Black Ch.
Loyola C, Md., 1852	Green, Gray Ch.
Loyola U of Los Angeles, Calif., 1911	Gray, Crimson Ch.
Loyola U, Ill., 1870	Maroon, Gold Ch.
Luther Theo Sem, Minn., 1876	Scarlet, Royal Blue Ch.
Lutheran Theo Sem, Penn., 1826	Navy Blue, Gold Ch.
Lutheran Theo Sem of Phila, Penn., 1864	No Hood
Lycoming C, Penn., 1812	Blue, Gold Ch.
Lynchburg C, Va., 1903	Crimson, Gray Ch.
Macalester C, Minn., 1874	Orange, Royal Blue Ch.
Mac Murray C, Ill., 1845	No Hood
Madison C, Va., 1908	Per Ch., Gold, Purple
Madonna C, Mich., 1947	Royal Blue, Old Gold Ch.
Maine, U of, Maine, 1865	Pale Blue
Malone C, Ohio, 1892	Red, White Ch.
Manchester C, Ind., 1889	Black, Gold Ch.

Manhattan Bible C, Kans., 1927 . . . . No Hood
Manhattan C, N. Y., 1853 . . . . . . White, Kelly Green Ch.
Manhattanville C of the Sacred Heart, N. Y., 1841 ... Maroon, White Ch.
Mankato St C, Minn., 1867 . . . . . . Purple, Gold Ch.
Mansfield St C, Penn., 1857 . . . . . . Red, Black Ch.
Marian C, Ind., 1937 . . . . . . Royal Blue, Gold Ch.
Marian C, Wis., 1936 . . . . Blue, White Ch.
Marion C, Ind., 1920 . . . . No Hood
Marist C, N. Y., 1946 . . . . Red, White Ch.
Maritime C, N. Y., (SUNY), 1874 . . . . Yale Blue, Maroon Ch.
Marietta C, Ohio, 1835 . . . . . Navy Blue, 4″ White Ch.
Marlboro C, Vt., 1946 . . . . . Dartmouth Green, Gold Ch.
Marshall U, W. Va., 1837 . . . . . Kelly Green, White Ch.
Mary Baldwin C, Va., 1842 . . . . . . Gold, White Ch.
Mary Manse C, Ohio, 1922 . . . . . Magenta, White Ch.
Marycrest C, Iowa, 1939 . . . . . Mary Blue, White Ch.
Marygrove C, Mich., 1910 . . . . . Gold, Kelly Green Ch.
Maryknoll Tchers C, N. Y., 1931 . . . . . No Hood
Maryland Inst., Md., 1826 . . . . . Yellow Gold, Black Ch.
Maryland, U of, Md., 1807 . . . . . Black, Old Gold Ch.
Marylhurst C, Oregon, 1893 . . . . . Royal Blue, Gold Ch.
Maryville C, Tenn., 1819 . . . . . Garnet, Orange Ch.
Maryville C of Sacred Heart, Mo., 1872 . . . . Red, White Ch.
Marymount C, Kans., 1922 . . . . . Royal Blue, White Ch.
Marymount C, Calif., 1948 . . White Velvet, White Satin Ch., Royal Blue
Massachusetts C of Art, Mass., 1873 . . . . . Blue, Gold Ch.
Mass. C of Optometry, Mass., 1909 . . . Maroon, Silver Gray Ch.
Massachusetts C of Pharmacy, Mass., 1823 . . . . Red, White Ch.
Mass. Inst of Tech., Mass., 1861 . . . Cardinal, Silver Gray Ch. Rev.
Massachusetts, U of, Mass., 1863 . . . . . Maroon, White Ch.
Mayville St Tchers C, N. Dak., 1889 . . . . . No Hood
McCormick Theo Sem, Ill., 1830 . . . . . Yale Blue, White Ch.
McKendree C, Ill., 1828 . . . . Royal Purple, Two White Chs.
McNeese St C, La., 1939 . . . . . . Gold, Purple Ch.
McPherson C, Kans., 1887 . . . . . Cerise Red, White Ch.
Medical C of South Carolina, S. C., 1823 . . . Gold, Black Ch.
Medical C of Virginia, Va., 1838 . . . . Myrtle Green, White Ch.
Medical Evangelists, C of . . . . . . See Loma Linda U
Menlo C, Calif., 1949 . . . . . . Royal Blue, White Ch.
Mercer U, Ga., 1833 . . . . . Orange, Two Black Chs. Rev.
Mercy C, Mich., 1941 . . . . . . White, Malta Blue Ch.
Mercyhurst C, Penn., 1926 . . . . . White, Kelly Green Ch.
Merrimack C, Mass., 1947 . . . . . Royal Blue, Gold Ch.
Miami U, Ohio, 1809 . . . . . . Crimson, White Ch.

Miami, U of, Fla., 1925 . . . . . Orange, White Ch. Green
Michigan C of Mining and Tech., Mich., 1885 . Medium Gold, Medium Silver Ch.
Michigan State U, Mich., 1885 . . Unofficial, Hunter Green, White Ch.
Michigan, U of, Mich., 1817 . . . . Maize, Azure Blue Ch.
Middle Tennessee St C, Tenn., 1911 . . . . Blue, White Ch.
Middlebury C, Vt., 1800 . . . . Yale Blue, White Ch.
Midland C, Nebr., 1887 . . . . Per Pale, Black, Orange
Midwestern U, Tex., 1922 . . . . Maroon, Old Gold Ch.
Midwestern Baptist Theo Sem, Mo., 1957 . . . Blue, Gold Ch.
Millersville St C, Penn., 1855 . . . . Gold, Three Black Chs.
Millikin U, Ill., 1901 . . . . Yale Blue, White Ch.
Mills C, Calif., 1852 . . . . . Gold, White Ch.
Mills C of Ed, N. Y., 1909 . . . Deep Purple, White Ch.
Milton C, Wis., 1867 . . . . . Blue, Brown Ch.
Milwaukee Sch of Engineering, Wis., 1903 . . Cardinal, White Ch.
Minnesota Bible C, Minn., 1913 . . . White, Royal Blue Ch.
Minnesota, U of, Minn., 1851 . . . Old Gold, Maroon Ch.
Minot St Tchers C, N. Dak. . . . . . No Hood
Misericordia, C, Penn., 1924 . . Dark Blue, Gold Ch. Rev., Light Blue
Mississippi Southern C, Miss., 1910 . . Spanish Yellow, Black Ch. Rev.
Mississippi St C for Women 1884 . . . . No Hood
Mississippi St U, Miss., 1878 . . . . White, Maroon Ch.
Mississippi, U of, Miss., 1844 . . . Crimson, Royal Blue Ch.
Missouri Sch of Religion, Mo., 1896 . . Per Ch., Kelly Green, Old Gold
Missouri, U of, Mo., 1843 . . . . Old Gold, Two Black Chs.
Missouri Valley C, Mo., 1889 . . . . Gold, Purple Ch.
Molloy Catholic C for Women, N. Y., 1955 . Bachelor of Arts Cerise, White Ch.
                                                    Bachelor of Science Cerise, Gold Ch.
Monmouth C, Ill., 1853 . . . . . Red, White Ch.
Monmouth C, N. J., 1933 . . . . Bachelor of Arts, Gold
                                                    Bachelor of Science, Blue, White Ch.
Montana Sch of Mines, Mont., 1893 . Copper, Narrow Dartmouth Green Ch.
Montana St C, Mont., 1893 . . . Royal Blue, Goldenrod Ch. Rev.
Montana St U, Mont., 1893 . . . Copper, Double Bar, Silver-Gold
Montclair St C, N. J., 1908 . . . . Scarlet, White Ch.
Moore Inst of Art, Penn., 1844 . . White, Dark Ivy Green Ch.
Moorhead St C, Minn., 1887 . . . . . Crimson
Moravian C, Penn., 1742 . . . . Navy Blue, Gray Ch.
Morehead St C, Ky., 1922 . . . . Royal Blue, Gold Ch.
Morgan St C, Md., 1867 . . . . Per Ch., Orange, Navy Blue
Morningside C, Iowa, 1894 . . . Maroon, White Ch. Rev.
Morris C, S. C., 1908 . . . . Royal Blue, Gold Ch.
Morris Harvey C, W. Va., 1888 . . . Maroon, Gold Ch.
Mt. Angel Sem, Oregon, 1889 . . . . Gold, White Ch. Rev.

Mount Holyoke C, Mass., 1837 . . . . Light Blue
Mount Marty C, S. D., 1935 . . . . White, Gold Ch.
Mount Mary C, Wis., 1913 . . . . Blue, White Ch.
Mount Mercy C, Iowa, 1928 . . . . . . Royal Blue, Gold Ch.
Mount St. Agnes C, Md., 1890 . . . . . . Garnet, Blue Ch.
Mount St. Joseph Tchers C, N. Y., 1937 . . . . . No Hood
Mt. St. Mary's C, Calif., 1925 . . . . . Purple, Gold Ch.
Mt. St. Mary's C, Md., 1808   Earned degrees...Light Blue
                        Honorary degrees...Per Ch., Light Blue, White
Mount St. Scholastica C, Kans., 1930 . . . . French Blue, White Ch.
Mount Union C, Ohio, 1846 . . . . . Royal Purple, White Ch.
Muhlenberg C, Penn., 1848 . . . . . Cardinal, Gray Ch.
Multnomah Sch of the Bible, Oreg., 1936 . . . . . Black
Mundelein C, Ill., 1929 . . . . . . Cardinal, Gold Ch.
Murray St C, Ky., 1922 . . . . . . Royal Blue, Old Gold Ch.
Muskingum C, Ohio, 1837 . . . . No Hood
Nashota House, Wis., 1842 . . . . See section on non-code hoods
Nasson C, Maine, 1912 . . . . . . Magenta, Gold Ch.
National C, Mo., 1899 . . . . No Hood
National C of Ed, Ill., 1886 . . . . Red
Nazareth C, Ky., 1920 . . . . . . Per Ch., White, Gold
Nazareth C of Rochester, N. Y., 1924 . . . Gold, Royal Purple Ch.
Nebraska, U of, Nebr., 1869 . . . . Per Ch., Scarlet, Cream
Nebraska Wesleyan U, Nebr., 1886 . . . . . No Hood
Nevada, U of, Nev., 1874 . . . . . Royal Blue, Silver Ch.
New Bedford Inst of Tech, Mass., 1895 . . . . Red, Gray Ch.
New Brunswick Theo Sem, N. J., 1784 . . . Blue, Orange Ch.
New England C, N. H., 1947 . . . . Scarlet, Royal Blue, Ch.
New England C of Pharmacy, Mass., 1948 . . . Blue, Gold Ch.
New England Cons of Music, Mass., 1867 . . Royal Blue, Old Gold Ch.
New Hampshire, U of, N. H., 1866 . . Per Ch., Royal Blue, White
New Mexico Highlands U, N. M., 1893 . . . Purple, White Ch.
New Mexico Inst of Mining and Tech, N. M., 1889 . . Silver, Gold Ch.
New Mexico St U, N. M., 1889 . . . . Crimson, White Ch.
New Mexico, U of, N. M., 1889 . . . Silver Gray, Cherry Red Ch.
New Mexico Western C, N. M., 1893 . . . . Purple, Gold Ch.
New Orleans Baptist Theo Sem, La., 1917 . . . Purple, Gold Ch.
New Paltz, C of Ed at, N. Y. (SUNY), 1886 . Royal Blue, Burnt Orange Ch.
New Rochelle, C at, N. Y., 1904 . . . Per Ch., Light Blue, White
New Sch for Social Research, N. Y., 1919 . . Emerald Green, White Ch.
New York, C of the City of . See City College of New York, Hunter College,
                               Brooklyn College, Queens College
New York Downstate Medical Center, N. Y., (SUNY), 1857 . Yale Blue, Gold Ch.
New York Maritime C . . . . See Maritime C

New York Medical C, N. Y., 1860 .   .   .   Gold, Crimson Ch. Rev.
New York, State U of .   .   .   .   .   .   See constituent elements
New York U, N. Y., 1831 .   .   .   .   Violet
New York, U of the St of (Regents), 1784 .   .   .   Purple, Gold Ch.
New York Upstate Medical Center, N. Y., (SUNY) 1950 .   Blue, Gold Ch.
Newark C of Engineering, N. J., 1881 .   .   .   Scarlet, White Ch.
Newark St C, N. J., 1855 .   .   .   Columbia Blue, Silver Gray Ch.
Newcomb C, La., 1886 .   .   .   .   Medium Brown, Light Blue Ch.
Newton Theo Inst, Mass., 1825 .   .   .   .   Purple, White Ch.
Niagara U, N. Y., 1856 .   .   .   .   .   .   Purple, White Ch.
Nicholls, F. T. St C, La., 1948 .   .   .   Rebel Red, Confederate Gray Ch.
North Adams St C, Mass., 1894 .   .   .   .   .   .   Gold
North Carolina Agr and Tech C, N. C., 1892 .   .   .   Royal Blue, Gold Ch.
North Carolina, U of, N. C., 1795 .   .   Columbia Blue, Two White Chs.
North Central C, Ill., 1861 .   .   .   .   .   .   No Hood
North Dakota Agr C, N. Dak. .   .   See North Dakota State University
North Dakota St U, N. Dak., 1890 .   .   Lemon Yellow, Grass Green Ch.
North Dakota, U of, N. Dak., 1883 .   .   .   .   Pink, Green Ch.
North Georgia C, Ga., 1873 .   .   .   .   Navy Blue, White Ch. Rev.
North Park C and Theo Sem, Ill., 1891 .   .   .   Royal Blue, Gold Ch.
North Texas, U of, Tex., 1890 .   .   .   .   Kelly Green, White Ch.
Northeast Missouri St Tchers C, Mo., 1867 .   .   White, Violet Purple Ch.
Northeastern St C, Okla., 1919 .   .   .   Kelly Green, White Ch. Rev.
Northeastern U, Mass., 1898 .   .   .   .   .   Cardinal, Black Ch.
Northern Baptist Theo Sem, Ill., 1913 .   .   Bright Red, Two White Chs.
Northern Illinois U, Ill., 1895 .   .   .   .   .   Cardinal, Black Ch.
Northern Michigan C, Mich., 1899 .   .   Olive Green, Two Gold Chs. Rev.
Northern St. Tchers C, S. Dak., 1901 .   .   .   .   Maroon, Gold Ch.
Northland C, Wis., 1891 .   .   .   .   Burnt Orange, Royal Blue Ch.
Northrop Inst of Tech, Calif., 1942 .   .   Royal Blue, Golden Yellow Ch.
Northwest Bible C, Wash., 1934 .   .   .   .   Gold, Royal Blue Ch.
Northwest Christian C, Oreg., 1895 .   .   .   .   Blue, Gold Ch.
Northwest Missouri St C, Mo., 1905 .   .   .   .   Green, White Ch.
Northwest Nazarene C, Idaho, 1913 .   .   .   .   Orange, Black Ch.
Northwestern Lutheran Sem, Minn., 1920 .   Per Pale, Bright Gold, Kelly Green
Northwestern St C, Okla., 1897 .   .   .   .   Cardinal, Black Ch.
Northwestern U, Ill., 1851 .   .   .   .   .   Purple, Gold Ch.
Norwich U, Vt., 1819 .   .   .   .   .   .   Maroon, Gold Ch.
Notre Dame C, Ohio, 1922 .   .   .   .   Royal Blue, Gold Ch.
Notre Dame, C of, Calif., 1851 .   .   .   .   Gold, White Ch.
Notre Dame C of Staten Island, N. Y., 1931 .   Bachelor of Arts...Blue, White Ch.
                              Bachelor of Science...Blue, Gold Ch.
Notre Dame of Maryland, C of, Md., 1895 .   .   .   Royal Blue, White Ch.
Notre Dame, U of, Ind., 1844 .   .   .   .   Per Ch., Old Gold, Royal Blue

Nyack Missionary C, N. Y., 1882 . . . . . Violet, White Ch.
Oakland City C, Ind., 1885 . . . . . Royal Blue, White Ch.
Oberlin C, Ohio, 1833 . . . . Cardinal, Two Mikado Yellow Chs.
Occidental C, Calif., 1887 . . . . . . Orange, Black Ch.
Ohio C of Chiropody, Ohio, 1916 . Honorary Degrees only...Royal Blue, Gold Ch.
                                Earned Degrees...see section on non-code hoods
Ohio Northern U, Ohio, 1871 . . . . No Hood
Ohio St U, Ohio, 1870 . . . . Scarlet, Gray Ch.
Ohio U, Ohio, 1804 . . . . . . Green, White Ch. Rev.
Ohio Wesleyan U, Ohio, 1842 . . . . . . Red, Black Ch.
Oklahoma Baptist U, Okla., 1910 . . . . . Green, Gold Ch.
Oklahoma City U, Okla., 1904 . . . . Royal Blue, White Ch.
Oklahoma C for Women, Okla., 1908 . . . . . No Hood
Oklahoma St U, Okla., 1890 . . . . . Orange, Black Ch.
Oklahoma, U of, Okla., 1890 . . . . . Crimson, Cream Ch.
Olivet C, Mich., 1844 . . . . . White, Bright Red Ch.
Olivet Nazarene C, Ill., 1908 . . . . . Purple, Gold Ch.
Omaha, U of, Nebr., 1908 . . . . . Maroon, Black Ch.
Oneonta, C of Ed at, N. Y., (SUNY) . . . Yale Blue, Gold Ch.
Orange County St C, Calif., 1959 . . . . . No Hood
Oregon St C, Oregon, 1858 . . . . . Burnt Orange
Oregon C of Ed, Oreg., 1882 . . . . . Crimson, Gray Ch.
Oregon, U of, Oreg., 1872 . . . Lemon Yellow, Emerald Green Ch.
Osteopathic Medicine and Surgery, C of, Iowa, 1898 . . Purple, White Ch.
Osteopathic Physicians and Surgeons, C of, Calif., 1914 . . Gold, Purple Ch.
Oswego, C of Ed at, N. Y., (SUNY) 1861 . . . Yale Blue, Gold Ch.
Ottawa U, Kans., 1865 . . . . . . Yellow, Black Ch.
Otterbein C, Ohio, 1847 . . . . . . Cardinal, Tan Ch.
Otis Art Inst, Calif., 1918 . . . . . See section on non-code hoods
Our Lady of Cincinnati C, Ohio, 1935 . . . Royal Blue, White Ch.
Our Lady of the Snows Scholasticate, Mo., 1953 . . Per Pale, Blue, White
Owosso C, Mich., 1909 . . . . Blue, Gold Ch.
Pace C, N. Y., 1906 . . . . . Per Bar, Gold, Royal Blue
Pacific Bible Sem, Calif., 1929 . . . . Green, Gold Ch., White
Pacific Lutheran Theo Sem, Calif. . . . Olive Green, Gold Ch. Rev.
Pacific Lutheran U, Wash., 1890 . . . . . Black, Gold Ch.
Pacific Oaks Friends Sch, Calif. . . . . . No Hood
Pacific Union C, Calif., 1909 . . . Bright Gold, Kelly Green Ch.
Pacific U, Oreg., 1849 . . . . . . Black, Scarlet Ch.
Pacific, U of the, Calif., 1851 . . . . Burnt Orange, Black Ch.
Pan American C, Tex., 1927 . . . . Forest Green, White Ch.
Panhandle A and M C, Okla., 1909 . . . . . No Hood
Park C, Mo., 1875 . . . . Wine, Canary Ch.
Pasadena C, Calif., 1902 . . . . . Kelly Green, Gold Ch.

Passionist Monastic Sem, N. Y., 1929 . . . . . . No Hood
Paterson St C, N. J., 1855 . . . . . . Orange, Black Ch.
Peabody Inst of the City of Baltimore, Md., 1868 . Cardinal Red, Navy Blue Ch.
Pembroke C, R. I., 1891 . . . . See Brown U
Pennsylvania St C of Optometry, Penn., 1919 . . . Black, White Ch.
Pennsylvania St U, Penn., 1855 . . . . . Dark Blue, White Ch.
Pennsylvania, U of, Penn., 1740 . . . . . . Red, Blue Ch.
Peru St Tchers C, Nebr., 1867 . . . . . Pale Blue, White Ch.
Pfeiffer C, N. C., 1885 . . . . Gold, Black Ch.
Philadelphia C of Bible, Penn., 1913 . . . . . Red, White Ch.
Philadelphia C of Optometry, Penn., 1898 . . . Maroon, Silver Gray Ch.
Philadelphia C of Pharmacy and Science, Penn., 1821 . . Blue, White Ch.
Philadelphia Divinity Sch . . . . See Divinity Sch in Philadelphia
Philadelphia Museum C of Art, Penn., 1876 . . . Cardinal, White Ch.
Phillips U, Okla., 1906 . . . . Maroon, White Ch.
Pikeville C, Ky., 1889 . . . . Black, Gold Ch.
Pittsburgh Theo Sem, Penn., 1794 . . . Old Gold, Three Purple Chs.
Pittsburgh, U of, Penn., 1787 . . . . . Navy Blue, Gold Ch.
Plattsburg, C of Ed at, N. Y., (SUNY), 1889 . . . Cardinal, White Ch.
Plymouth Tchers C, N. H., 1870 . . . Dartmouth Green, White Ch.
Polytechnic Inst of Brooklyn, N. Y., 1854 . . . Purple Navy, Gray Ch.
Pomona C, Calif., 1887 . . . . . Navy Blue (Light), White Ch.
Portland St C, Oreg., 1955 . . . . No Hood
Portland, U of, Oreg., 1935 . . . . . . Purple, White Ch.
Potsdam, C of Ed at, N. Y., (SUNY), 1869 . . . . Red, Gray Ch.
Prairie View A and M C, Texas, 1876 . Per Ch., Royal Purple, Old Gold Ch.
Pratt Inst, N. Y., 1887 . . . . Cadmium Yellow
Presbyterian Sch of Christian Ed, Va., 1914 . . . Green, White Ch.
Princeton Theo Sem, N. J., 1812 . . . . Cardinal, Royal Blue Ch.
Princeton U, N. J., 1746 . . . . . . Orange, Black Ch.
Principia C, Ill., 1932 . . . . No Hood
Providence C, R. I., 1917 . . . . . . White, Black Ch.
Puerto Rico, U of, P. R., 1903 . . . . . Scarlet, White Ch.
Purdue U, Ind., 1869 . . . . . Black, Two Old Gold Chs.
Puget Sound, U of, Wash., 1888 . . . . Maroon, White Ch.
Queens C, N. Y., 1937 . . . . . . Royal Blue, Silver Ch.
Quincy C, Ill., 1873 . . . . Van Dyke Brown
Radcliffe C, Mass., 1879 . . . . . . Crimson, White Ch.
Radford C, Va., 1910 . . . . . . Gray, Purple Ch. Rev.
Randolph-Macon Women's C, Va., 1891 . . . Lemon, Black Ch.
Redlands, U of, Calif., 1907 . . . . . Maroon, Gray Ch.
Reed C, Oreg., 1909 . . . . . Richmond Red, White Ch.
Regis C, Colo., 1877 . . . . Brown, Gold Ch.

Reformed Episcopal Church, Theo Sem of, Penn., 1886 . . Navy Blue,
                                                            Cadet Gray Ch. Rev.
Regis C, Mass., 1927 . . . . . . Crimson, Two Gold Chs.
Rensselear Polytechnic Inst, N. Y., 1824 . . Bright Cherry Red, White Ch.
Rhode Island C, R. I., 1854 . . . . Gold, White Ch.
            An edging of Blue overlaps the Gold, one of Gold overlaps the White
Rhode Island Sch of Design, R. I., 1877 . . . Maroon, Light Gray Ch.
Rhode Island, U of, R. I., 1892 . . . . White, R. I. Blue Ch.
Rice U, Tex., 1891 . . . . Blue, Gray Ch.
Ricker C, Maine, 1926 . . . . . . Purple, Gold Ch.
Rider C, N. J., 1865 . . . . Purple, Gold Ch.
Rio Grande C, Ohio, 1876 . . . . . Red, Two White Chs.
River Falls St C, Wis., 1874 . . . . No Hood
Rivier C, N. H., 1933 . . . . . . Royal Blue, Silver Ch.
Roanoke C, Va., 1853 . . . Mandarin Yellow, National Blue Ch.
Roberts Wesleyan C, N. Y., 1866 . . . . Scarlet, White Ch.
Rochester Inst of Tech, N. Y., 1829 . . . Royal Blue, Gray Ch.
Rochester, U of, N. Y., 1850 . . . . Dandelion Yellow
Rockefeller Inst, N.Y., 1901 . . Golden Yellow, Two Royal Blue Chs.
Rockford C, Ill., 1847 . . . . Purple, White Ch.
Rollins C, Fla., 1885 . . . . . . Per Ch., Yale Blue, Gold
Roosevelt U, Ill., 1945 . . . . . Veridian Green, White Ch.
Rosary C, Ill., 1848 . . . . Light Blue
Rosary Hill C, N. Y., 1947 . . . . Copenhagen Blue, Ivory Ch.
Rose Polytechnic Inst, Ind., 1874 . . . . Old Rose, White Ch.
Rosemont C, Penn., 1922 . . . . . . Rose, Gray Ch.
Rutgers, The St U, N. J., 1766 . . . . Scarlet
Sacred Heart C, Kans., 1933 . . . . . Per Ch., Red, Blue
Sacred Heart, C of the, P. R., 1935 . . . . . Red, Gold Ch.
Sacred Heart Dominican C, Tex., 1946 . . . . Red, Old Gold Ch.
St Anselm's C, N. H., 1889 . . . . . Dark Blue, White Ch.
St Augustine's C, N. C., 1867 . . . . No Hood
St Basil's C, Conn., 1939 . . . . . . Sky Blue, White Ch.
St Benedict, C of, Minn., 1913 . . . . . Red, White Ch. Rev.
St Benedict's C, Kans., 1858 . . . . . Black, White Ch.
St Bernadine of Sienna C, N. Y., 1938 . . . Forest Green, Gold Ch. Rev.
St Bernard C, Ala., 1892 . . . . . Royal Blue, White Ch.

St Bonaventure U, N. Y., 1923 . . { Bachelors—Brown, Two White Chs.
                                   { Masters—Per Ch., Brown, White
                                   (Doctors—Brown, White Ch.

St Catherine, C of, Minn., 1906 . . . . Royal Purple, Old Gold Ch.
St Edward's U, Tex., 1885 . . . . . Old Gold, Navy Blue Ch.
St Francis, C of, Ill., 1920 . . . . . . Gold, Brown Ch.
St Francis C, Ind., 1940 . . . . . . White, Blue-Green Ch.

St Francis C, Maine, 1943 . . . . Crimson, Gold Ch.
St Francis C, N. Y., 1884 . . . . . Royal Blue, Scarlet Ch.
St John C, Ohio, 1928 . . . . Red, Gold Ch.
St John Fisher C, N. H., 1951 . . . Per Bar, Gold, Cardinal
St John's C, Md., 1784 . . . . See section on non-code hoods
St John's Sem, Mass., 1884 . . . . No Hood
St John's U, Minn., 1857 . . . . . Cardinal, Blue Ch.
St Joseph C, Conn., 1925 . . . Medium Blue, Medium Gold Ch.
St Joseph on the Rio Grande, C of, N. M., 1940 . Royal Blue, Two Gold Chs. Rev.
St Joseph's C, Ind., 1889 . . . . . Cardinal, Purple Ch.
St Joseph's C, Penn., 1851 . . . . . . Crimson, Gray Ch.
St Joseph's C for Women, N. Y., 1916 . . . Old Gold, White Ch.
St Lawrence U, N. Y., 1856 . . Scarlet, Medium Dark Brown Ch.
St Louis Inst of Music, Mo., 1924 . . . . Maroon, Gold Ch.
St Louis U, Mo., 1818 . . . . . White, Yale Blue Ch.
St Margaret's House, Calif., 1914 . . Ice Blue, Royal Blue Ch.
St Martin's C, Wash., 1895 . . . Per Ch., Red, White
St Mary C, Kans., 1923 . . . . . Gold, White Ch.
St Mary of the Plains C, Kans., 1952 . . White, Royal Blue Ch. Rev.
St Mary of the Springs, C of, Calif., 1911 . . Gold, Black Ch. White
St Mary of the Woods C, Ind., 1840 . . Medium Blue, White Ch.
St Mary's C, Ind., 1844 . . . . Light Blue, White Ch.
St Mary's C, Ky., 1821 . . . . No Hood
St Mary's C, Mich., 1885 . . . . . Red, White Ch.
St Mary's C, Minn., 1874 . . . . . Red, White Ch.
St Mary's C of California, Calif., 1863 . . Cardinal Red, Royal Blue Ch.
St Mary's Dominican C, La., 1910 . . . . . . White
St Mary's Sem and U, Md., 1791 . Pale Blue, Triple Ch., Gold, White, Black
St Mary's U, Tex., 1852 . . . . Yale Blue, Yellow Gold Ch.
St Meinrad Sem, Ind., 1861 . . . . . . No Hood
St Michael's C, Vt., 1904 . . . . . Gold, Purple Ch.
St Norbert C, Wis., 1898 . . Per Pale, White, Green—Yellow Ch.
St Olaf C, Minn., 1887 . . . . Black, Old Gold Ch.
St Pius X Sem, N. Y., 1956 . . . . . . No Hood
St Rose, C of, N. Y., 1920 . . . . . Gold, White Ch.
St Scholastica, C of, Minn., 1924 . . Royal Purple, Two Gold Chs.
St Teresa, C of, Minn., 1907 . . . . White, Gold Ch.
St Teresa, C of, Mo., 1940 . . . . Gold, Purple Ch.
St Thomas, C of, Minn., 1885 . . . . Purple, Gray Ch.
St Thomas, U of, Tex., 1947 . . . . Scarlet, Gold Ch.
St Vincent C, Penn., 1846 . . . Forest Green, Yellow Gold Ch.
St Xavier C, Ill., 1847 . . . . . Gray, Crimson Ch.
Salem C, N. C., 1772 . . . . Per Ch., Yellow, White
Salem C, W. V., 1888 . . . . Olive Green, White Ch. Rev.

Salmon P. Chase C, Ohio, 1893 . . . . . Maroon, White Ch.
Salve Regina C, R. I., 1934 . . . . . . Blue, White Ch.
Sam Houston St Tchers C, Tex., 1879 . . Blue, White Ch., Burnt Orange
San Diego C for Women, Calif., 1949 . . . Per Ch., Old Gold, Scarlet
San Diego St C, Calif., 1950 . . . . . Scarlet, Black Ch.
San Diego, U of, C for Men, Calif., 1949 . . . . White, Delft Ch.
San Fernando Valley St C, Calif., 1958 . . . . Red, White Ch.
San Francisco C for Women, Calif., 1930 . . . . Old Gold, Red Ch.
San Francisco Cons of Music, Calif., 1922 . . . United Nations Blue
San Francisco St C, Calif., 1899 . . . . . Purple, Gold Ch.
San Francisco Theo Sem, Calif., 1871 . Scarlet, Golden Yellow Ch., Royal Blue
San Francisco, U of, Calif., 1855 . . . . . Kelly Green, Gold Ch.
San Jose St C, Calif., 1857 . . . . . Golden Yellow, White Ch.
San Luis Rey C, Calif., 1940 . . . . No Hood
Santa Clara, U of, Calif., 1851 . . . . . Per Ch., Cardinal, White
Sarah Lawrence C, N. Y., 1926 . . . Emerald Green, White Ch. Rev.
Savannah St C, Ga., 1890 . . . . No Hood
Scarrit C for Christian Workers, Tenn., 1892 . . . Green, White Ch.
Scranton, U of Pa., 1888 . . . . . Royal Purple, White Ch.
Scripps C, Calif., 1926 . . . Sage Green, Deep V-shaped Silver Stripe
Seabury Western Theo Sem, Ill., 1858 . . . Gray, Red Ch., Purple
Seat of Wisdom C, Conn. . . . . . . No Hood
Seattle Pacific C, Wash., 1891 . . . . Maroon, Two White Chs.
Seattle U, Wash., 1891 . . . . . Maroon, White Ch.
Seneca, Colleges of . . . . See Hobart C and William Smith C
Seton Hall U, N. J., 1861 . . . . . . Yale Blue, White Ch.
Seton Hill C, Penn., 1883 . . . . . Per Ch., Crimson, Gold
Shelton C, N. J., 1885 . . . . . . Purple, Old Gold Ch.
Shimer C, Ill., 1853 . . . . . Maroon, Three Gold Chs.
Shorter C, Ark., 1885 . . . . . Navy Blue, Old Gold Ch.
Siena Heights C, Mich., 1919 . . . . White, Old Gold Ch.
Simmons C, Mass., 1899 . . . . . Royal Blue, Gold Ch.
Sinclair C, Ohio, 1887 . . . . . . Maroon, Gray Ch.
Skidmore C, N. Y., 1911 . . . . . Yellow, White Ch.
Slippery Rock St C, Penn., 1889 . . . Kelly Green, White Ch.
Smith C, Mass., 1871 . . . . . . White, Gold Ch.
South Carolina St C, S. C., 1896 . . . . Maroon, Blue Ch.
South Carolina, U of, S. C., 1801 . . . . Garnet, Black Ch.
South Dakota Sch of Mines, 1885 . . . . Gold, Silver Ch.
South Dakota St C, S. D., 1881 . . . Light Blue, Two Yellow Chs.
South Dakota, St U of, S. Dak., 1882 . . . . . Red
South Texas C, Tex., 1923 . . . . . . No Hood
Southeastern Baptist Theo Sem . . . . . . No Hood

Southeastern Bible C, Ala., 1935 . . . White, Two Scarlet Chs.
Southern Baptist Theo Sem, Ky., 1859 . . . . Crimson, White Ch.
Southern California C, Calif., 1920 . . . Royal Blue, Gold Ch.
Southern California Sch of Theo, Calif., 1885 . Gray, Harvard Crimson Ch.
Southern California, U of, Calif., 1880 . . . Gold, Cardinal Ch.
Southern Connecticut St C, Conn., 1893 . . Connecticut Blue, White Ch.
Southern Illinois U, Ill., 1869 . . . . Maroon, White Ch.
Southern Methodist U, Tex., 1911 . . . . . Blue, Red Ch.
Southern Oregon C, Oreg., 1926 . . . Vermilion, Sand Yellow Ch.
Southern St C, Ark., 1909 . . . . Royal Blue, Old Gold Ch.
Southern St Tchers C, S. Dak., 1881 . . . . . No Hood
Southern U, La., 1880 . . . . . . Gold, Blue Ch.
Southern Utah, C of, Utah, 1897 . . . . Navy Blue, White Ch.
Southwestern at Memphis, Tenn., 1848 . . Per Ch., Cardinal, Black
Southwestern Baptist Theo Sem, Tex., 1908 . . . Royal Blue, White Ch.
Southwestern Bible Inst, Tex., 1944 . . . Purple, Gold Ch. Rev.
Southwestern Louisiana, U of, La., 1900 . . Vermilion Red, White Ch.
Southwestern St C, Okla., 1955 . . . . Navy Blue, White Ch.
Southern U, Tex., 1840 . . . . . Per Ch., Old Gold, Black
Spring Hill C, Ala., 1830 . . . . Deep Violet, White Ch.
Springfield C, Mass., 1885 . . . . Maroon, White Ch.
Stanford U, Calif., 1885 . . . . . . Cardinal
State C at . . . . . . See location of college
State U of . . . . . See state except New York, State U of
State Tchers C . . . . . . See location or state
State U of New York (SUNY) . . . See constituent elements
Stephen F. Austin St C, Texas, 1923 . . . . Purple, White Ch.
Stetson U, Fla., 1883 . . . . . Emerald Green, White Ch.
Steubenville, C of, Ohio, 1946 . . . Old Gold, Three Kelly Green Chs.
Stevens Point St C, Wis., 1894 . . . . . . No Hood
Stevens Inst of Tech, N. J., 1870 . . . . Gray, Red Ch.
Stout St C, Wis., 1893 . . . . . White, Royal Blue Ch.
Sul Ross St C, Tex., 1920 . . . . . Scarlet, Gray Ch.
Superior St C, Wis., 1896 . . . . . Orange, Black Ch.
Susquehanna U, Penn., 1858 . . . . Maroon, Two Orange Chs.
Swarthmore C, Penn., 1864 . . . . . . Garnet
Sweet Briar C, Va., 1901 . . . . Dark Green, Pale Pink Ch.
Syracuse U, N. Y., 1870 . . . . Orange
Talbot Theo Sem, Calif., 1952 . . . . White, Two Red Chs.
Tarkio C, Miss., 1883 . . . . . Purple, Cream Ch.
Taylor U, Ind., 1846 . . . . Old Gold, Three Deep Purple Chs.
Temple U, Penn., 1888 . . . . . White, Cherry Ch.
Tennessee A and Indus. St U, Tenn., 1912 . . . Royal Blue, White Ch.
Tennessee Polytechnic Inst, Tenn., 1915 . . . Purple, Old Gold Ch.

Tennessee, U of, Tenn., 1794 . . . . . . Gold, White Ch.
Texas, A and M C of, Tex., 1871 . . . . Maroon, White Ch.
Texas C, Tex., 1894 . . . . . . Purple, Gold Ch. Rev.
Texas C of Arts and Industries, Tex., 1925 . . Per Ch., Blue, Gold
Texas Southern U, Tex., 1947 . . . . . Maroon, Gray Ch.
Texas Technological C, Tex., 1923 . . . . Scarlet, Black Ch.
Texas, U of, Texas, 1881 . . . . . . Orange, White Ch.
Texas Wesleyan U, Texas, 1891 . . . . Gold, Royal Blue Ch.
Texas Western C, Tex., 1913 . . Masters Degrees—Per Ch., Orange, White
                        Bachelors Degrees—White, Two Orange Chs.
Texas Woman's University, Tex., 1902 . . . Maroon, White Ch.
Textile Tech Inst of, Va., 1947 . . . . Mauve, Crimson Ch.
Thiel C, Pa., 1866 . . . . Blue, Gold Ch.
Tiffin U, Ohio, 1918 . . . . Green, Gold Ch.
Toccoa Falls Bible C, Ga., 1911 . . . . . . No Hood
Toledo, U of, Ohio, 1872 . . . . . Dark Blue, Gold Ch.
Tougaloo Southern Christian C, Miss., 1869 . See section on non-code hoods
Towson St Tchers C, Md., 1866 . . . Per Bar, Yellow Gold, White
Transylvania College, Ky., 1780 . . . . . . Crimson
Trevecca Nazarene C, Tenn., 1935 . . . . Purple, White Ch.
Trenton St C, N. J., 1855 . . . . Dark Blue, Gold Ch. Rev.
Trinity College, Conn., 1823 . . . See section on non-code hoods
Trinity C, D. C., 1897 . . . . Purple, Gold Ch.
Trinity C, Ill., 1897 . . . . . Royal Blue, Two White Chs.
Trinity C, Vt., 1925 . . . . . . Baby Blue, Silver Ch.
Trinity Theo Sem . . . . . . See Trinity College, Ill.
Trinity U, Tex., 1869 . . . . . Maroon, Broad White Ch.
Tri-State C, Ind., 1884 . . . . . . Azure, White Ch.
Tufts C, Mass., 1852 . . . . . . Brown, Blue Ch.
Tulane U, La., 1834 . . . . . Olive Green, Light Blue Ch.
Tulsa, U of, Okla., 1894 . . Old Gold, Double Ch. Crimson-Royal Blue
Tuskegee Institute, Ala., 1881 . . . . . Crimson, Gold Ch.
Union C, Ky., 1879 . . . . Orange, Black Ch.
Union C, N. Y., 1795 . . . . Garnet
Union U, Tenn., 1825 . . . . . . Cardinal, Cream Ch.
Union Theo Sem, N. Y., 1836 . . . . . . Scarlet
Union Theo Sem in Virginia, 1812 . . . Alice Blue, White Ch.
United States Merchant Marine Academy, N. Y., 1938 . . . No Hood
United States Military Academy, N. Y., 1802 . Official description is "three equal
    vertical parts of gray, gold and black, in that order ... from inside to outside."
    Diagram sent was Gray, Gold Ch. Rev, Black.
United States Naval Academy, Md., 1845 . . . . . No Hood
United Theo Sem, Ohio, 1871 . . . . . Crimson, Yale Blue Ch.
University of . . . . See key word

Upland C, Calif., 1920 . . . . . Maroon, Gray Ch.
Upper Iowa U, Iowa, 1857 . . . . Per Bar, Peacock Blue, White
Upsala C, N. J., 1893 . . . . . Yale Blue, Silver Gray Ch.
Ursuline C, Ky., 1938 . . . . . Maroon, White Ch.
Ursinus College, Pa., 1869 . . . . Red, Old Gold Ch., Black
Utah, U of, Utah, 1850 . . . . . Red, White Ch.
Valdosta St C, Ga., 1906 . . . . Red, Black Ch.
Valley City St Tchers C, N. Dak., 1890 . . . . No Hood
Valparaiso U, Ind., 1859 . . . . Old Gold, Brown Ch.
Vanderbilt U, Tenn., 1873 . . . . Gold, Black Ch.
Vassar C, N. Y., 1861 . . . . . Rose, Gray Ch. Rev.
Venard C, Iowa, 1910 . . . . . Purple, White Ch.
Vermont, U of, Vt., 1791 . . . . Green, Gold Ch.
Villa Madonna C, Ky., 1921 . . . Per Ch., Royal Blue, White
Villanova C, Pa., 1842 . . . . Navy Blue, Two White Chs.
Virginia Military Institute, Va., 1839 . . . . No Hood
Virginia Polytechnic Institute, Va., 1872 . . . Orange, Maroon Ch.
Virginia St C, Va., 1882 . . . . Blue, Orange Ch.
Virginia Theo Sem, and C, Va., 1888 . . . Royal Blue, White Ch.
Virginia, U of, Va., 1819 . . . . Navy Blue, Orange Ch.
Viterbo C, Wis., 1931 . . . . . Gray, Rose Ch.
Wabash C, Ind., 1832 . . . . . Scarlet
Wagner C, Staten Island, N. Y., 1883 . . . Dartmouth Green, White Ch.
Walla Walla C, Wash., 1892 . . . Forest Green, Burnt Orange Ch.
Warner Pacific C, Oregon, 1937 . . . . No Hood
Wartburg C, Iowa, 1852 . . . . Black, Three Orange Chs.
Washburn U of Topeka, Kans., 1865 . . . . Yale Blue
Washington and Jefferson C, Penn., 1781 . . . Per Ch., Red, Black
Washington C, Md., 1782 . . . . Maroon, Black Ch.
Washington Missionary C, Md., 1904 . . . White, Royal Blue Ch.
Washington St U, Wash., 1889 . . . Per Ch., Crimson, Silver Gray
Washington U, Mo., 1853 . . . . Green, Red Ch.
Washington, U of, Wash., 1861 . . . Per Ch., Purple, Gold
Washington and Lee U, Va., 1749 . . . Blue, Two White Chs. Rev.
Wayland Baptist C, Tex., 1908 . . . Royal Blue, Gold Ch.
Wayne St Tchers C, Neb., 1910 . . . . Gold, Black Ch.
Wayne St U, Mich., 1868 . . . Forest Green, Old Gold Ch.
Waynesburg C, Penn., 1849 . . . . Orange, Black Ch.
Webb Inst of Naval Arch., N. Y., 1889 . . . Medium Blue, White Bar
Webster C, Mo., 1915 . . . . . Gold, White Ch.
Wellesley C, Mass., 1870 . . . . Yale Blue, White Ch.
Wells C, N. Y., 1868 . . . . . Cardinal
Wesley Theo Sem, D. C., 1881 . . . . Purple, White Ch.
Wesleyan C, Ga., 1836 . . . . Purple, Lavender Ch.

Wesleyan U, Conn., 1831 . . . . . Cardinal, Black Ch.
West Chester St C, Penn., 1871 . . . . . Purple, Gold Ch.
West Texas St C, Tex., 1910 . . . . Maroon
West Virginia U, W. Va., 1867 . . . Per Ch., Old Gold, Navy Blue
West Virginia Wesleyan C, W. Va., 1890 . . . Burnt Orange, Black Ch.
Western Carolina C, N. C., 1889 . . . . Purple, Two Gold Chs.
Western C for Women, Ohio, 1853 . . . . . . Yale Blue
Western Evangelical Sem, Ore., 1945 . . . . Green, White Ch.
Western Illinois U, Ill., 1899 . . . . . Purple, Gold Ch.
Western Kentucky St C, Ky., 1906 . . . . Scarlet, White Ch.
Western Maryland C, Md., 1867 . . . Olive Green, Old Gold Ch.
Western Michigan U, Mich., 1903 . . . Seal Brown, Old Gold Ch.
Western Montana C of Ed, Mont., 1893 . . . Orange, Black Ch.
Western New England C, Mass., 1919 . . . . Blue, Gold Ch.
Western Ontario, U of, Ont., 1878—
    All degrees except Ph.D., Purple, Two White Chs.
    Ph.D., Purple hood lined White piped Purple
Western Reserve U, Ohio, 1826 . . . . . White, Scarlet Ch.
Western St C of Colorado, Colo., 1911 . . . Crimson, Slate Ch.
Western Theo Sem, Mich., 1866 . . Per Bar, California Gold, Royal Blue
Western Washington St C, Wash., 1893 . . . Royal Blue, White Ch.
Westfield, St C at, Mass., 1838 . . . . Light Blue, White Ch.
Westminster Choir C, N. J., 1926 . . . Royal Purple, Gold Ch.
Westminster C, Mo., 1851 . . . . . . Royal Blue
Westminster C, Penn., 1852 . . . . . Per Ch., White, Blue
Westminster C, Utah, 1875 . . . . . . Purple, Gold Ch.
Westminster Theo Sem, Pa., 1929 . . . . . . Royal Blue
Wheaton C, Ill., 1860 . . . . Deep Orange, Two Dark Blue Chs.
Wheelock C, Mass., 1888 . . . . . . Gold, White Ch.
Whitewater St C, Wis., 1868 . . . . . Purple, White Ch.
Whitman C, Wash., 1859 . . . . . . Blue, Maize Ch.
Whittier C, Calif., 1901 . . . . . Purple, Bright Gold Ch.
Whitworth C, Wash., 1890 . . . . . Red, Black Ch. Rev.
Wichita, U of, Kans., 1895 . . . . Sunflower Yellow, Black Ch.
Wilberforde U, Ohio, 1856 . . . . . . Gold, Green Ch.
Wiley C, Tex., 1873 . . . . Purple, White Ch.
William and Mary, C of, Va., 1693 . Bottle Green, U.S. Army Silver Gray Ch., Gold
William Jewell C, Mo., 1849 . . . . Cardinal, Black Ch. Rev.
William Mitchell C of Law, Minn., 1900 . . . . . Sky Blue
William Smith C, N. Y., 1822 . . . . . . Evergreen
Willamette U, Oreg., 1842 . . . . . Cardinal, Gold Ch.
Williams C, Mass., 1793 . . . . Purple
Willimantic St C, Conn., 1889 . . . . Connecticut Blue, White Ch.
Wilmington C, Ohio, 1870 . . . . . Kelly Green, White Ch.

Winona St C, Minn., 1858 . . . . Purple, White Ch.
Winthrop C, S. C., 1886 . . . . Garnet, Gold Ch.
Wisconsin Cons, Inc., Wis., 1899 . . . . . . No Hood
Wisconsin, U of, Wis., 1849 . . . . Cardinal
Wittenberg U, Ohio, 1845 . . . . . . Scarlet, White Ch.
Woman's C of Georgia, Ga., 1889 . . Cocoa Brown, Live Medium Gold Ch.
Women's Medical C of Pennsylvania, Penn., 1850 . Silver Gray, Scarlet Ch.
Woodstock C, Md., 1869 . . . . Gold, White Ch.
Worcester Polytechnic Inst, Mass., 1865 . . . Gray, Crimson Ch.
Worcester, St C at, Mass., 1871 . . . Royal Blue, Yellow Gold Ch.
Wyoming, U of, Wyoming, 1887 . . . . Brown, Yellow Ch.
Xavier U, Ohio, 1831 . . . . . . Navy Blue, Two White Chs.
Yale U, Conn., 1701 . . . . Yale Blue
Yeshiva U, N. Y., 1886 . . . . Sky Blue
Youngstown U, Ohio, 1908 . . . . . Cardinal, White Ch.

Institutions — Hoods
1. Single Color Hood Lining

1a. *Black*

Black . . . . . . Multnomah School of the Bible, Oreg.

1b. *White or Silver*

White . . . . Bowdoin College Maine
White . . . . . . Long Island University, N. Y. (B.A. only)
White . . . . . . St. Mary's Dominican College, La.

1c. *Yellow or Gold*

Cadmium Yellow . . . . . . Pratt Institute, N. Y.
Dandelion Yellow . . . . . Rochester, University of, N. Y.
Dark Gold . . . . Beloit College, Wis.
Gold . . . . . . California Podiatry College, Calif.
Gold . . . . Long Island University, N. Y. (B.A. only)
Gold . . . . . . North Adams State College, Mass.
Gold . . . . . . Monmouth College, N. J. (B.A. only)
Old Gold . . . . . Drexel Institute of Technology, Pa.
Old Gold . . . Eastern Montana College of Education, Mont.
Old Gold . . . . DePauw University, Ind.
Old Gold . . . . . Fort Hayes Kansas State College, Kans.
Old Gold . Hebrew Union College—Jewish Institute of Religion, N. Y. and Ohio
Old Gold . . . . . . Iowa, State University of, Iowa
Saffron . . . Boston Conservatory of Music, Mass. (B.F.A. only)

1d. *Red*

Blood Red . . . . Florida Southern College, Fla.
Bright Red . . . Kirksville College of Osteopathy and Surgery, Mo.
Cardinal . . . . Fairfield University, Conn.
Cardinal . . . . Louisville, University of, Ky.
Cardinal . . . . Stanford University, Calif.
Cardinal . . . . Wells College, N. Y.
Cardinal . . . . Wisconsin, University of, Wis.
Cardinal, Dark (Small gray chevron on each side, hidden), Chapman College, Calif.
Crimson . . . . Bridgewater State College, Mass.
Crimson . . . . Moorhead State College, Minn.
Crimson . . . . Transylvania College, Ky.
Garnet . . . . Bates College, Maine
Garnet . . . . Swarthmore College, Pa.
Garnet . . . . Union College, N. Y.
Maroon . . . . Chicago, University of, Ill.
Maroon . . . . Fordham University, N. Y.
Maroon . . . . La Crosse State College, Wis.
Maroon . . . . West Texas State College, Tex.
Pink . . . Boston Conservatory of Music, Mass. (B.Mus., M.Mus. only)
Red . . . . Davidson College, N. C.
Red . . . . National College of Education, Ill.
Red . . . . South Dakota, St. University of, S. Dak.
Scarlet . . . . . . Rutgers, The State University, N. J.
Scarlet . . . . Union Theo Sem, N. Y.
Scarlet . . . . Wabash College, Ind.

1e. *Blue*

Blue . . . . Connecticut College, Conn.
Electric Blue . . . . Andover Theo Sem, Mass.
Light Blue . . Cathedral College of the Immaculate Conception, N. Y.
Light Blue . . . . . . Livingston State College, Ala.
Light Blue . . . . . . Mount Holyoke College, Mass.
Light Blue . . . Mount St. Mary's College, Md. (earned degrees)
Light Blue . . . . Rosary College, Ill.
Pale Blue . . . . Maine, University of, Maine
Royal Blue . . . . Westminster College, Mo.
Royal Blue . . . . Westminster Theo Sem, Pa.
Royal Midnight Blue . . . . . . Bennington College, Vt.
Sky Blue . . . . . William Mitchell College of Law, Minn.
Sky Blue . . . . Yeshiva University, N. Y.
United Nations Blue . . . San Francisco Conservatory of Music, Calif.
Wedgewood Blue . . . . Brandeis University, Mass.

Yale or Connecticut Blue	. . . . .	Danbury State College, Conn.
Yale Blue	. . . . . .	Gordon Divinity School, Mass.
Yale Blue	. . . .	Washburn University of Topeka, Kans.
Yale Blue	. . . . .	Western College for Women, Ohio
Yale Blue	. . . .	Yale University, Conn.

1f. *Orange*

Burnt Orange	. . . . .	Chouinard Art Institute, Calif.
Burnt Orange	. . . . .	Oregon State College, Oreg.
Cadmium Orange	. . . . .	Baker University, Kans.
Orange	. . . . . .	Syracuse University, N. Y.

1g. *Purple*

Lavender	. . . . .	City College of New York, N. Y.
Mauve	. . . . . .	Kenyon College, Ohio
Purple	. . . . . .	Williams College, Mass.
Royal Purple	. . . .	Holy Cross, College of the, Mass.
Violet	. . . . . .	New York University, N. Y.

1h. *Green*

Dark Green	. . . . .	Dartmouth College, N. H.
Evergreen	. . . . . .	William Smith College, N. Y.
Seafoam Green	. . . .	Chicago College of Osteopathy, Ill.

1i. *Brown*

Van Dyke Brown	. . . . . .	Quincy College, Ill.

2. *Single Chevron*

Field	Chevron	Institution

2ab. *Black with White Chevron*

Field		Chevron		Institution
Black	. . . .	White	. . .	Penna State College of Optometry, Pa.
Black	. . . .	White	. . . .	St. Benedict's College, Kans.

2ac. *Black with Yellow or Gold Chevron*

Field		Chevron		Institution
Black	. . . .	Gold	. .	Appalachian State Teachers College, N. C.
Black	. . . .	Gold	. . .	Colorado College, Colo.
Black	. . . .	Gold	. . .	Manchester College, Ind.
Black	. . . .	Gold	. .	Pacific Lutheran College, Wash.
Black	. . . .	Gold	. . . .	Pikeville College, Ky.
Black	. . . .	Old Gold	. . .	Harding College, Ark.
Black	. . . .	Old Gold	. .	Johns Hopkins University, Md.
Black	. . . .	Old Gold	. . .	Maryland, University of, Md.
Black	. . . .	Old Gold	. . . .	St. Olaf College, Minn.
Black	. . . .	Yellow	. .	Frostburg State Teachers College, Md.

2ad. *Black with Red Chevron*

Black . . . . Scarlet . . . . . Pacific University, Oreg.

2ae. *Black with Blue Chevron*

Black . . . . Baby Blue . Jefferson Medical College of Philadelphia, Pa.

2af. *Black with Orange Chevron*

Black . . . . Orange . . . . . Greenville College, Ill.

2ba. *White or Silver with Black Chevrons*

White . . . . Black . . . . . Dominican College, Wis.
White . . . . Black . . . . . Providence College, R. I.

2bc. *White or Silver with Gold Chevron*

Silver . . . . Gold . New Mexico Inst of Mining and Tech., N. Mex.
White . . . . Gold . . . . Centre College of Kentucky, Ky.
White . . . . Gold . . . . St. Teresa College of, Minn.
White . . . . Gold . . . . . . Smith College
White . . . . Old Gold . . . Mount Marty College, S. Dak.
White . . . . Old Gold . . . Siena Heights College, Mich.

2bd. *White or Silver with Red Chevron*

White . . . . Bright Red . . . . . Olivet College, Mich.
White . . . . Cherry . . . . . Temple University, Pa.
White . . . . Maroon . . . Eastern Kentucky State College, Ky.
White . . . . Maroon . . Mississippi State University, Miss.
White . . . . Red . . . . . D'Youville College, N. Y.
White . . . . Scarlet . . . Christian Brothers College, Tenn.
White . . . . Scarlet . . . Western Reserve University, Ohio

2be. *White or Silver with Blue Chevron*

White . . . . Delft . San Diego University of, College for Men, Calif.
White . . . . Malta Blue . . . . . Mercy College, Mich.
White . . . . Rhode Island Blue . Rhode Island, University of, R. I.
White . . . . Royal Blue . . . Culver-Stockton College, Mo.
White . . . . Royal Blue . . . Minnesota Bible College, Minn.
White . . . . Royal Blue . . . . Stout State College, Wis.
White . . . . Royal Blue . Washington Missionary College, Md.
White . . . . Yale Blue . . . Albertus Magnus College, Conn.
White . . . . Yale Blue . . . Dubuque, University of, Iowa
White . . . . Yale Blue . . . . St. Louis University, Mo.

2bf. *White or Silver with Orange Chevron*

White . . . . Orange . . . . . Carroll College, Wis.

2bg. *White or Silver with Purple Chevron*

White . . . . Violet Purple . Northeast Missouri St Tchers C, Mo.

2bh. *White or Silver with Green Chevron*

White . . . . Blue-Green . . . . St. Francis College, Ind.
White . . . . Dark Ivy Green . . . Moore Institute of Art, Pa.
White . . . . Emerald Green . . . . Clark University, Mass.
White . . . . Green . . . . Loretto Heights College, Colo.
White . . . . Kelly Green . . . . Manhattan College, N. Y.
White . . . . Kelly Green . . . . Mercyhurst College, Pa.

2bxx. *White or Silver top with Chevron and different color bottom*

Top	Chevron	Bottom	Institution
White velvet	White satin	Royal Blue Satin	. Marymount College, Calif.
White	Blue	Red	. Holy Trinity Orthodox Seminary, N. Y.

2ca. *Yellow or Gold with Black Chevron*

Field	Chevron	Institution
Bright Gold . .	Black	Gustavus Adolphus College, Minn.
Gold . . .	Black	Adrian College, Mich.
Gold	Black	Doane College, Nebr.
Gold	Black	Harris Teachers College, Mo.
Gold	Black . . .	Los Angeles State College, Calif.
Gold	Black . .	Medical College of South Carolina, S. C.
Gold	Black . . .	Wayne State Teachers College, Nebr.
Gold	Black	Pfeiffer College, N. C.
Gold	Black	Vanderbilt University, Tenn.
Lemon	Black . .	Randolph-Macon Women's College, Va.
Old Gold . . .	Black . . .	Birmingham-Southern College, Ala.
Sunflower Yellow .	Black	Wichita, University of, Kans.
Yellow	Black	Ottawa University, Kans.
Yellow Gold . .	Black	Maryland Institute, Md.

2cb. *Yellow or Gold with White or Silver Chevron*

Gold . . . . Silver . . . South Dakota Sch of Mines, S. Dak.
Gold . . . . White . . . Catholic University of America, D. C.
Gold . . . . White . Dominican College of San Rafael, Calif.
Gold . . . . White . . . . Mary Baldwin College, Va.
Gold . . . . White . . . . . Mills College, Calif.
Gold . . . . White . . . Notre Dame, College of, Calif.
Gold . . . . White . . . . Rhode Island College, R. I.
Gold . . . . White . . . . St. Mary College, Kans.
Gold . . . . White . . . . Saint Rose, College of, N. Y.
Gold . . . . White . . . Tennessee, University of, Tenn.

Gold	White	Webster College, Mo.
Gold	White	Wheelock College, Mass.
Gold	White	Woodstock College, Md.
Golden Yellow	White	Cedar Crest College, Pa.
Golden Yellow	White	San Jose State College, Calif.
Medium Gold	Medium Silver	Michigan College of Mining and Technology, Mich.
Old Gold	White	Bryn Mawr College, Pa.
Old Gold	White	Geneva College, Pa.
Old Gold	White	Georgia Institute of Technology, Ga.
Old Gold	White	St. Joseph's College for Women, N. Y.
Yellow	White	Skidmore College, N. Y.
Yellow Gold	White	Grace College, Ind.

2cd. *Yellow or Gold with Red Chevron*

Gold	Cardinal	Southern California, University of, Calif.
Old Gold	Maroon	Minnesota, University of, Minn.
Old Gold	Red	San Francisco College for Women, Calif.
Yellow	Maroon	Colgate-Rochester Divinity School, N. Y.
Yellow	Red	Evangelical Congregational Sch of Theology, Pa.
Yellow Gold	Crimson	Kansas State College of Pittsburg, Kans.

2ce. *Yellow or Gold with Blue Chevron*

Gold	Admiral Blue	John C. Smith University, N. C.
Gold	Blue	Alderson-Broaddus College, Va.
Gold	Blue	Southern University, La.
Gold	Royal Blue	Alaska, University of, Alaska
Gold	Royal Blue	Arizona State College, Ariz.
Gold	Royal Blue	Bethel College and Seminary, Minn.
Gold	Royal Blue	John Herron Art School, Ind.
Gold	Royal Blue	Northwest Bible College, Wash.
Gold	Royal Blue	Texas Wesleyan University, Tex.
Gold	Yale Blue	California, University of, Calif.
Maize	Blue (Azure)	Michigan, University of, Mich.
Maize	Royal Blue	Carleton College, Minn.
Mandarin Yellow	National Blue	Roanoke College, Va.
Old Gold	Blue	Eau Claire State College, Wis.
Old Gold	Blue	Graceland College, Iowa
Old Gold	Navy Blue	La Salle College, Pa.
Old Gold	Navy Blue	St. Edward's University, Tex.
Old Gold	Navy Blue	U. S. Naval Academy, Md. (Unofficial)
Old Gold	Royal Blue	Chattanooga, University of, Tenn. (Bachelors only)
Old Gold	Royal Blue	Kearney State Teachers College, Nebr.

2cg. *Yellow or Gold with Purple Chevron*

Gold	. . . .	Purple	. . . .	Converse College, S. C.
Gold	. . . .	Purple	. . . .	Fontbonne College, Mo.
Gold	. . . .	Purple	. . .	Golden Gate Baptist Theo Sem, Calif.
Gold	. . . .	Purple	. . . .	Houghton College, N. Y.
Gold	. . . .	Purple	. . .	Loma Linda University, Calif.
Gold	. . . .	Purple	. .	Los Angeles College of Optometry, Calif.
Gold	. . . .	Purple	. . .	McNeese State College, La.
Gold	. . . .	Purple	. . .	Missouri Valley College, Mo.
Gold	. . . .	Purple	.	Osteopathic Physicians and Surgeons, College of, Calif.
Gold	. . . .	Purple	. . . .	St. Michael's College, Vt.
Gold	. . . .	Purple	. . . .	St. Teresa, College of, Mo.
Gold	. . . .	Royal Purple	.	Nazareth College of Rochester, N. Y.
Old Gold	. . .	Purple	. . .	Colorado State College, Colo.

2ch. *Yellow or Gold with Green Chevron*

Bright Gold	. . .	Kelly Green	. . .	Pacific Union College, Calif.
Copper	. . . .	Dartmouth Green (Narrow chevron)		Montana School of Mines, Mont.
Gold	. . . .	Kelly Green	. . .	Marygrove College, Mich.
Gold	. . . .	Green	. . . .	Wilberforce University, Ohio
Lemon Yellow	. .	Emerald Green	. .	Oregon, University of, Oreg.
Lemon Yellow	. .	Grass Green	.	North Dakota State University, N. Dak.
Pumpkin Yellow	.	Alfalfa Green	. .	Colorado State University, Colo.

2ci. *Yellow or Gold with Brown Chevron*

Gold	. . . .	Brown	. . . .	Adelphi College, N. Y.
Gold	. . . .	Brown	. . . .	Glassboro State College, N. J.
Gold	. . . .	Brown	. . .	Long Beach State College, Calif.
Gold	. . . .	Brown	. . . .	St. Francis, College of, Ill.
Old Gold	. . .	Brown	. . . .	Alverno College, Wis.
Old Gold	. . .	Brown	. . . .	Valparaiso University, Ind.

2cj. *Yellow or Gold with Gray Chevron*

Gold	. . . .	Silver Gray	. . .	Colorado, University of, Colo.

2cxx. *Gold top with Chevron and different color bottom*

Top	Chevron	Bottom	Institution
Gold	. . Black	. . White	. St. Mary of the Springs, College of, Ohio

2da. *Red with Black Chevron*

Field	Chevron	Institution
Cardinal	. . . Black	. . . . Northeastern University, Mass.
Cardinal	. . . Black	. . . . Northern Illinois University, Ill.

Cardinal . . .	Black	Northwestern State College, Okla.
Cardinal . . .	Black	Wesleyan University, Conn.
Cardinal . . .	Black	William Jewell College, Mo.
Garnet	Black . . .	South Carolina, University of, S. C.
Maroon	Black	Omaha, University of, Nebr.
Maroon	Black	Washington College, Md.
Old Rose . . .	Black	Blackburn College, Ill.
Red	Black	Arkansas State College, Ark.
Red	Black . . .	Central Missouri State College, Mo.
Red	Black	Haverford College, Pa.
Red	Black	Judson College, Ala.
Red	Black . . .	East Stroudsburg State College, Pa.
Red	Black	La Grange College, Ga.
Red	Black . . .	Lowell Technological Institute, Mass.
Red	Black	Mansfield State College, Pa.
Red	Black . . .	Ohio Wesleyan University, Ohio
Red	Black	Valdosta State College, Ga.
Scarlet	Black	San Diego State College, Calif.
Scarlet	Black	Texas Technological College, Tex.

2db. *Red with White or Silver Chevron*

Cardinal . . .	Cream	Union University, Tenn.
Cardinal . . .	White	Arkansas, University of, Ark.
Cardinal . . .	White	Cardinal Cushing College, Mass.
Cardinal . . .	White	Chico State College, Calif.
Cardinal . . .	White	Keene Teachers College, N. H.
Cardinal . . .	White . .	Lamar State College of Technology, Tex.
Cardinal . . .	White . .	Milwaukee School of Engineering, Wis.
Cardinal . . .	White . . .	Philadelphia Museum C of Art, Pa.
Cardinal . . .	White .	Plattsburg, State College of Ed, N. Y. (SUNY)
Cardinal . . .	White	Youngstown University, Ohio
Cerise Red . . .	White	McPherson College, Kans.
Cerise	White .	Molloy Catholic College for Women, N. Y. (B.A. only)
Cherry Red (Bright)	White . . .	Rensselaer Polytechnic Institute, N. Y.
Crimson . . .	Cream	Indiana University, Ind.
Crimson . . .	Cream	Oklahoma, University of, Okla.
Crimson . . .	White	Alabama, University of, Ala.
Crimson . . .	White	Belmont Abbey College, N. C.
Crimson . . .	White	Bible, College of, Ky.
Crimson . . .	White	Carthage College, Ill.
Crimson . . .	White	Cascade College, Oreg.
Crimson . . .	White	Holy Names, College of the, Calif.
Crimson . . .	White	Miami University, Ohio

Crimson	White	New Mexico State University, N. Mex.
Crimson	White	Radcliffe College, Mass.
Crimson	White	Southern Baptist Theo Sem, Ky.
Magenta	White	Mary Manse College, Ohio
Maroon	White	Baltimore, University of, Md.
Maroon	White	Claremont Men's College, Calif.
Maroon	White	Earlham College, Ind.
Maroon	White	Fairleigh Dickinson University, N. J.
Maroon	White	Manhattanville, College of the Sacred Heart, N. Y.
Maroon	White	Massachusetts, University of, Mass.
Maroon	White	Phillips University, Okla.
Maroon	White	Puget Sound, University of, Wash.
Maroon	White	Salmon P. Chase College, Ohio
Maroon	White	Seattle University, Wash.
Maroon	White	Southern Illinois University, Ill.
Maroon	White	Springfield College, Mass.
Maroon	White	Texas, Agricultural and Mechanical College, Tex.
Maroon	White	Texas Woman's University, Tex.
Maroon	White (Broad)	Trinity University, Tex.
Maroon	White	Ursuline College, Ky.
Old Rose	White	Rose Polytechnic Institute, Ind.
Red	White	Alliance College, Pa.
Red	White	Ball State Teachers College, Ind.
Red	White	Bradley University, Ill.
Red	White	Cana College, Nebr.
Red	White	Dana College, Nebr.
Red	White	Denison University, Ohio
Red	White	Detroit College of Law, Mich.
Red	White	Dickinson School of Law, Pa.
Red	White	Eastern Washington State College, Wash.
Red	White	Eastern Nazarene College, Mass.
Red	White	Edinboro State College, Pa.
Red	White	Farmington State Teachers College, Maine
Red	White	Malone College, Ohio
Red	White	Marist College, N. Y.
Red	White	Maryville College of the Sacred Heart, Mo.
Red	White	Massachusetts College of Pharmacy, Mass.
Red	White	Monmouth College, Ill.
Red	White	Philadelphia College of Bible, Pa.
Red	White	St. Mary's College, Mich.
Red	White	St. Mary's College, Minn.
Red	White	San Fernando Valley State College, Calif.
Red	White	Utah, University of, Utah
Richmond Red	White	Reed College, Oreg.

Scarlet	Silver . . .	Conservative Baptist Theo Sem, Colo.
Scarlet	White	Austin Peay State College, Tenn.
Scarlet	White	Bard College, N. Y.
Scarlet	White	Boston University, Mass.
Scarlet	White	Central College, Iowa
Scarlet	White	Curtis Institute of Music, Pa.
Scarlet	White	Dickinson College, Pa.
Scarlet	White	Hartford, University of, Conn.
Scarlet	White	Illinois State Normal University, Ill.
Scarlet	White	Lincoln Bible Institute, Ill.
Scarlet	White	Montclair State College, N. J.
Scarlet	White . . .	Newark College of Engineering, N. J.
Scarlet	White . .	Puerto Rico, University of, Puerto Rico
Scarlet ' . . .	White . . .	Roberts Wesleyan College, N. Y.
Scarlet	White . . .	Western Kentucky State College, Ky.
Scarlet	White	Wittenberg University, Ohio
Vermilion Red . .	White .	Southwestern Louisiana, University of, La.

2dc. *Red with Gold Chevron*

Cardinal . . .	Gold	Mundelein College, Ill.
Cardinal . . .	Gold	Willamette University, Oreg.
Cerise . . .	Gold . .	Molloy Catholic College for Women, N. Y.
		(B.S. only)
Crimson . . .	Gold	Austin College, Tex.
Crimson . . .	Gold	Central High School of Phila., Pa.
Crimson . . .	Gold	Denver, University of, Colo.
Crimson . . .	Gold	Ferris Institute, Mich.
Crimson . . .	Gold	Good Counsel College, N. Y.
Crimson . . .	Gold	St. Francis College, Maine
Crimson . . .	Gold	Tuskegee Institute, Ala.
Garnet . . .	Gold	Florida State University, Fla.
Garnet . . .	Gold	Winthrop College, S. C.
Magenta . . .	Gold	Nasson College, Maine
Maroon, Medium .	Bright Gold .	Bloomfield College and Seminary, N. J.
Maroon . . .	Gold	Arizona State University, Ariz.
Maroon . . .	Gold	Bethune-Cookman College, Fla.
Maroon . . .	Gold	Bloomsburg State College, Pa.
Maroon . . .	Gold	Boston College, Mass.
Maroon . . .	Gold	Calvin College, Mich.
Maroon . . .	Gold . . .	Central Michigan University, Mich.
Maroon . . .	Gold	Concordia Teachers College, Ill.
Maroon . . .	Gold	Cooper Union, N. Y.
Maroon . . .	Gold	Elon College, N. C.
Maroon . . .	Gold	Gannon College, Pa.

Maroon	.	.	.	Gold	.	.	.	.	Golden Gate College, Calif.
Maroon	.	.	.	Gold	.	.	.	Kutztown State College, Pa.
Maroon	.	.	.	Gold	.	.	.	.	Loyola University, Ill.
Maroon	.	.	.	Gold	.	.	Morris Harvey College, W. Va.
Maroon	.	.	.	Gold	.	Northern State Teachers College, S. Dak.
Maroon	.	.	.	Gold	.	.	.	Norwich University, Vt.
Maroon	.	.	.	Gold	.	.	St. Louis Institute of Music, Mo.
Maroon	.	.	.	Old Gold	.	.	Midwestern University, Tex.
Red	.	.	.	Gold	.	.	.	.	.	King's College, Pa.
Red	.	.	.	Gold	.	Sacred Heart, College of, Puerto Rico
Red	.	.	.	Gold	.	.	.	.	St. John College, Ohio
Red	.	.	.	Old Gold	.	Sacred Heart Dominican College, Tex.
Scarlet	.	.	.	Gold	.	.	.	Lancaster Theo Sem, Pa.
Scarlet	.	.	.	Gold	.	St. Thomas, University of, Tex.
Scarlet	.	.	.	Old Gold	.	.	Cabrini College, Radnor, Pa.
Vermilion	.	.	.	Sand Yellow	.	Southern Oregon College, Oreg.
Wine	.	.	.	Canary	.	.	.	.	Park College, Mo.

2de. *Red with Blue Chevron*

Cardinal	.	.	.	Blue	.	.	.	.	St. John's University, Minn.
Cardinal	.	.	Navy Blue	.	Peabody Inst of the City of Baltimore, Md.
Cardinal	.	.	Royal Blue	.	.	.	Fresno State College, Calif.
Cardinal	.	.	Royal Blue	.	.	.	.	Lane College, Tenn.
Cardinal	.	.	Royal Blue	.	Louisiana Polytechnic Institute, La.
Cardinal	.	.	Royal Blue	.	.	.	Princeton Theo Sem, N. J.
Cardinal	.	.	Royal Blue	.	St. Mary's College of California, Calif.
Carmine	.	.	Ultramarine	.	.	.	Armstrong College, Calif.
Cherry Red	.	.	Sky Blue	.	.	.	Hiram College, Ohio
Crimson	.	.	Navy Blue	.	.	.	Hanover College, Ind.
Crimson	.	.	Royal Blue	.	.	.	Howard College, Ala.
Crimson	.	.	Royal Blue	.	Mississippi, University of, Miss.
Crimson	.	.	Yale Blue	.	.	.	United Theo Sem, Ohio
Garnet	.	.	.	Blue	.	.	.	Mount St. Agnes College, Md.
Garnet	.	.	.	Turquoise	.	George Peabody College for Tchers, Ed. D.
Harvard Crimson	.	Yale Blue	.	.	Kansas, University of, Kans.
Maroon	.	.	.	Blue	.	.	.	.	King College, Tenn.
Maroon	.	.	.	Blue	.	South Carolina State College, S. C.
National Red	.	.	Blue	.	.	.	Arizona, University of, Ariz.
Red	.	.	.	Blue	.	.	Pennsylvania, University of, Pa.
Red	.	.	.	Light Blue	.	.	Dayton, University of, Ohio
Scarlet	.	.	.	Royal Blue	.	.	Julliard School of Music, N. Y.
Scarlet	.	.	.	Royal Blue	.	.	.	Luther Theo Sem, Minn.
Scarlet	.	.	.	Royal Blue	.	.	New England College, N. H.

2df. *Red with Orange Chevron*
Garnet . . . . Orange . . . . . Maryville College, Tenn.

2dg. *Red with Purple Chevron*
Cardinal . . . Purple . . . . . St. Joseph's College, Ind.

2dh. *Red with Green Chevron*
Pink . . . . Green . . . North Dakota, University of, N. Dak.

2di. *Red with Brown Chevron*
Cardinal . . . Tan . . . . . . Otterbein College, Ohio
Scarlet . . . . (Medium) Brown . . St. Lawrence University, N.Y

2dj. *Red with Gray Chevron*
Cardinal . . . Gray . . . . Indiana Central College, Ind.
Cardinal . . . Gray . . . . Muhlenberg College, Pa.
Crimson . . . Gray . . . . . Atlanta University, Ga.
Crimson . . . Gray . . . . . Fenn College, Ohio
Crimson . . . Gray . . . . Lynchburg College, Va.
Crimson . . . Gray . . Oregon College of Education, Oreg.
Crimson . . . Gray . . . . St. Joseph's College, Pa.
Crimson . . . Slate . . Western State College of Colorado, Colo.
Maroon . . . Gray . . . . . Concord College, Va.
Maroon . . . Gray . . . Redlands, University of, Calif.
Maroon . . . Gray . . . . Sinclair College, Ohio
Maroon . . . Gray . . . Texas Southern University, Tex.
Maroon . . . Gray . . . . . Upland College, Calif.
Maroon . . . Light Gray . . Rhode Island School of Design, R. I.
Maroon . . . Silver Gray . Massachusetts College of Optometry, Mass.
Maroon . . . Silver Gray . Philadelphia College of Osteopathy, Pa.
Maroon . . . Slate . . . . . Indiana State College, Pa.
Rainwine (Maroon) Silver Gray . Henderson State Teachers College, Ark.
Rebel Red . . . Confederate Gray . Nicholls, F. T., State College, La.
Red . . . . Gray . . New Bedford Institute of Technology, Mass.
Red . . . . Gray . Potsdam College of Education, N.Y. (SUNY)
Rose . . . . Gray . . . . . Rosemont College, Pa.
Scarlet . . . Gray . . . . . Beaver College, Pa.
Scarlet . . . Gray . . . . Ohio State University, Ohio
Scarlet . . . Gray . . . Sul Ross State College, Tex.
Scarlet . . . Pearl Gray . . . Bellarmine College, Ky.
Scarlet . . . Silver Gray . . Illinois Institute of Technology, Ill.

2dxx. *Red top with Chevron and different color bottom*

Top	Chevron	Bottom	Institution
Red	White	Blue	American University, D. C.
Red	Old Gold	Black	Ursinus College, Pa.
Scarlet	Golden Yellow	Royal Blue	San Francisco Theo Sem, Calif.

2eb. *Blue with White or Silver Chevron*

Field	Chevron	Institution
Alice Blue	White	Union Theo Sem in Virginia, Va.
Azure	White	Tri-State College, Ind.
Baby Blue	Silver	Trinity College, Vt.
Biarritz Blue	White	Georgian Southern College, Ga.
Blue	Silver	Berry College, Ga.
Blue	White	Crozer Theological Seminary, Pa.
Blue	White	Elmhurst College, Ill.
Blue	White	Gonzaga University, Wash.
Blue	White	Indiana State College, Ind.
Blue	White	Kentucky, University of, Ky.
Blue	White	Marian College, Wis.
Blue	White	Middle Tennessee State College, Tenn.
Blue	White	Monmouth College, N. J. (B.S. only)
Blue	White	Mount Mary College, Wis.
Blue	White	Notre Dame College of Staten Island, N. Y. (A.B. only)
Blue	White	Philadelphia College of Pharmacy and Science, Pa.
Blue	White	Salve Regina College, R. I.
Connecticut Blue	White	Southern Connecticut State College, Conn.
Connecticut Blue (Azure)	White	Williamantic State College, Conn.
Copenhagen Blue	Ivory	Rosary Hill College, N. Y.
Dark Blue	White	Pennsylvania State University, Pa.
Dark Blue	White	St. Anselm's College, N. H.
French Blue	White	Mount St. Scholastica College, Kans.
Light Blue	White	Catholic University of Puerto Rico, Puerto Rico
Light Blue	White	Citadel The, S. C.
Light Blue	White	Columbia University, N. Y.
Light Blue	White	Iliff School of Theology, Colo.
Light Blue (Columbia)	White	Immaculata College, Pa.
Light Blue	White	Jewish Theo Sem of America, N. Y.
Light Blue	White	St. Mary's College, Ind.
Light Blue	White	Westfield State College, Mass.
Mary Blue	White	Marycrest College, Iowa
Medium Blue	White	St. Mary of the Woods College, Ind.
National Flag Blue	White	Connecticut, University of, Conn.
Navy Blue	White	Bethany Biblical Seminary, Ill.
Navy Blue	White	Dallas, University of, Tex.
Navy Blue	White	Marietta College, Ohio
Navy Blue	White	Southern Utah, College of, Utah

Navy Blue	White	Southwestern State College, Okla.
Navy Blue, Light	White	Pomona College, Calif.
Pale Blue	White	Peru State Teachers College, Nebr.
Royal Blue	Silver	Nevada, University of, Nev.
Royal Blue	Silver	Rivier College, N. H.
Royal Blue	Silver	Queens College, N. Y.
Royal Blue	White	Anna Maria College for Women, Mass.
Royal Blue	White	Atlantic Christian College, N. C.
Royal Blue	White	Aurora College, Ill.
Royal Blue	White	Azusa College, Calif.
Royal Blue	White	Baptist Bible Seminary, N. Y.
Royal Blue	White	Bob Jones University, S. C.
Royal Blue	White	Butler University, Ind.
Royal Blue	White	Central Bible Institute and Seminary, Mo.
Royal Blue	White	Central Connecticut State College, Conn.
Royal Blue	White	Chaminade College of Honolulu, Hawaii
Royal Blue	White	Cheney State College, Pa.
Royal Blue	White	Concordia Teachers College, Nebr.
Royal Blue	White	Concordia Theo Sem, Ill.
Royal Blue	White	Dakota Wesleyan University, S. Dak.
Royal Blue	White	Drake University, Iowa
Royal Blue	White	Duke University, N. C.
Royal Blue	White	Eastern Baptist Theo Sem, Pa.
Royal Blue	White	Eastern Pilgrim College, Pa.
Royal Blue	White	Fayetteville State Teachers College, N. C.
Royal Blue	White	Franklin University, Ohio
Royal Blue	White	Hartwick College, N. Y.
Royal Blue	White	Hillsdale College, Mich.
Royal Blue	White	Howard University, D. C.
Royal Blue	White	Lebanon Valley College, Pa.
Royal Blue	White	Longwood College, Va.
Royal Blue	White	Marymount College, Kans.
Royal Blue	White	Menlo College, Calif.
Royal Blue	White	Notre Dame of Maryland, College of, Md.
Royal Blue	White	Oakland City College, Ind.
Royal Blue	White	Oklahoma City University, Okla.
Royal Blue	White	Our Lady of Cincinnati College, Ohio
Royal Blue	White	St. Bernard College, Ala.
Royal Blue	White	Southwestern Baptist Theo Sem, Tex.
Royal Blue	White	Tennessee A & I State University, Tenn.
Royal Blue	White	Virginia Theo Sem and College, Va.
Royal Blue	White	Western Washington State College, Wash.
Sky Blue	White	St. Basil's College, Conn.
Virgin Blue	White	Holy Family College, Wis.

Yale Blue	White	Berea College, Ky.
Yale Blue	White	Buffalo, University of, N. Y.
Yale Blue	White	Catawba College, N. C.
Yale Blue	White	Franklin and Marshall College, Pa.
Yale Blue	White	McCormick Theo Sem, Ill.
Yale Blue	White	Middlebury College, Vt.
Yale Blue	White	Milikin University, Ill.
Yale Blue	White	Seton Hall University, N. J.
Yale Blue	White	Wellesley College, Mass.

2ec. *Blue with Gold or Yellow Chevron*

Azure Blue	Gold	Great Falls, College of, Mont.
(Continental) Blue	(Continental) Buff	Hamilton College, N. Y.
Blue	Gold	Allen University, S. C.
Blue	Gold	Augustana Theo Sem, Ill.
Blue	Gold	Blue Mountain College, Miss.
Blue	Gold	East Texas State College, Tex.
Blue	Gold	Emory University, Ga.
Blue	Gold	Goucher College, Md.
Blue	Gold	Hahnemann Medical College, Pa.
Blue	Gold	Lycoming College, Pa.
Blue	Gold	Massachusetts College of Art, Mass.
Blue	Gold	Midwestern Baptist Theo Sem, Mo.
Blue	Gold	New England College of Pharmacy, Mass.
Blue	Gold	(New York) Upstate Medical Center, N. Y. (SUNY)
Blue	Gold	Northwest Christian College, Oreg.
Blue	Gold	Notre Dame College of Staten Island, N. Y. (B.S. only)
Blue	Gold	Owosso College, Mich.
Blue	Gold	Thiel College, Pa.
Blue	Gold	Western New England College, Mass.
Blue	Golden Yellow	Delaware, University of, Del.
Blue	Maize	Whitman College, Wash.
Blue	Old Gold	Alleghany College, Pa.
Blue	Old Gold	Columbia Theo Sem, Ga.
Dark Blue	Buff	The George Washington University, D. C.
Dark Blue	Gold	Buena Vista College, Iowa
Dark Blue	Gold	Buffalo, College of Education at, N.Y. (SUNY)
Dark Blue	Gold	Ithaca College, N. Y.
Dark Blue	Gold	Toledo, University of, Ohio
Medium Blue	Gold	Central Wesleyan College, S. C.
Medium Blue	Medium Gold	St. Joseph College, Conn.
Navy Blue	Gold	Harpur College, N. Y. (SUNY)

Navy Blue . . .	Gold	Lutheran Theo Sem, Pa.
Navy Blue . . .	Gold	Pittsburgh, University of, Pa.
Navy Blue . . .	Old Gold	Akron, University of, Ohio
Navy Blue . . .	Old Gold . . .	Franklin College of Indiana, Ind.
Navy Blue . . .	Old Gold	George Fox College, Oreg.
Navy Blue . . .	Old Gold	Howard Payne College, Tex.
Navy Blue . . .	Old Gold	Shorter College, Ala.
Navy Blue . .	Yellow Gold . . .	John Carroll University, Ohio
Royal Blue . .	Antique Gold . . .	George Williams College, Ill.
Royal Blue . . .	Daffodil Yellow	Lander College, S. C.
Royal Blue . . .	Gold . . .	.Aroostock State Teachers College, Maine
Royal Blue . . .	Gold	Benedictine Heights College, Okla.
Royal Blue . . .	Gold	California Baptist Theo Sem, Calif.
Royal Blue . . .	Gold . . .	Dunbarton College of Holy Cross, D. C.
(Royal) Blue . .	Gold . . .	East Tennessee State College, Tenn.
Royal Blue . . .	Gold	Eastern Oregon College, Oreg.
Royal Blue . . .	Gold . . .	Grand Rapids Baptist Theo Sem and Bible Institute, Mich.
Royal Blue . . .	Gold	Hofstra College, N. Y.
Royal Blue . . .	Gold	Kansas City, University of, Mo.
Royal Blue . . .	Gold	Marian College, Ind.
Royal Blue . . .	Gold	Marylhurst College, Oreg.
Royal Blue . . .	Gold	Merrimack College, Mass.
Royal Blue . .	Gold (New) . . .	Moorhead State College, Ky.
Royal Blue . . .	Gold	Morris College, S. C.
Royal Blue . . .	Gold	Mount Mercy College, Iowa
Royal Blue . . .	Gold	(North Carolina) Agricultural and Technical College, N. C.
Royal Blue . . .	Gold . . .	North Park College and Theo Sem, Ill.
Royal Blue . . .	Gold	Notre Dame College, Ohio
Royal Blue . . .	Gold	Ohio College of Chiropody, Ohio (Honoraries only)
Royal Blue . .	Gold	Simmons College, Mass.
Royal (Blue) . .	Gold . . .	Southern California College, Calif.
Royal Blue . . .	Gold	Wayland Baptist College, Tex.
Royal Blue . . .	Gold Yellow .	Geneseo College of Ed (SUNY), N. Y.
Royal Blue . . .	Golden Yellow .	Northrop Inst of Technology, Calif.
Royal Blue . . .	Old Gold . . .	Chicago-Kent College of Law, Ill.
Royal Blue . . .	Old Gold . . .	East Texas Baptist College, Tex.
Royal Blue . . .	Old Gold . . .	John Brown University, Ark.
Royal Blue . . .	Old Gold	Madonna College, Mich.
Royal Blue . . .	Old Gold	Murray State College, Ky.
Royal Blue . . .	Old Gold .	New England Conservatory of Music, Mass.
Royal Blue . . .	Old Gold	Southern State College, Ark.

Royal Blue . . . Yellow Gold . . Worcester, State College at, Mass.
Turquoise . . . Gold . . . M. J. Lewi College of Podiatry, N. Y.
Yale Blue . . . Gold . . . . . . Dropsie College, Pa.
Yale Blue . . . Gold . Fredonia, State College of Ed at (SUNY), N. Y.
Yale Blue . . . Gold . . . New York Downstate Medical Center (SUNY), N. Y.
Yale Blue . . . Gold . . . . Oneonta, College of Education at, (SUNY), N. Y.
Yale Blue . . . Gold . . . Oswego, College of Education at, (SUNY), N. Y.
Yale Blue . . . Old Gold . . . . . Juniata College, Pa.
Yale Blue . . . Yellow Gold . . . . . St. Mary's U, Tex.

2ed. *Blue with Red Chevron*

Blue . . . . Red . . . . . De Paul University, Ill.
Blue . . . . Red . . . Southern Methodist University, Tex.
Navy Blue . . . Crimson . . . . Bangor Theo Sem, Maine
Royal Blue . . . Scarlet . . . . . St. Francis College, N. Y.
Turquoise . . . Garnet . George Peabody C for Tchers, Tenn., Ed.S.
Yale Blue . . . Maroon . Maritime College, State University of New York, N. Y.

2ee. *Blue with Blue Chevron*

Ice Blue . . . . Royal Blue . . . Saint Margaret's House, Calif.

2ef. *Blue with Orange Chevron*

Blue . . . . Orange . . . New Brunswick Theo Sem, N. J.
Blue . . . . Orange . . . . Virginia State College, Va.
Navy Blue . . . Burnt Orange . . . . Lincoln University, Pa.
Navy Blue . . . Orange . . . . Virginia, University of, Va.
Royal Blue . . . Burnt Orange . . New Paltz, College of Education at (SUNY), N. Y.

2eh. *Blue with Green Chevron*

Oxford Blue . . Lincoln Green . Drew University, N. J. (All except B.A.)

2ei. *Blue with Brown Chevron*

Blue . . . . Brown . . . . . Milton College, Wis.

2ej. *Blue with Gray Chevron*

Blue . . . . Gray . . . . . Elizabethtown College, Pa.
Blue . . . . Gray . Lincoln Memorial University, Tenn. (Unoff)
Blue . . . . Gray . . . . . Rice University, Tex.
Columbia Blue . Silver Gray . . . . Newark State College, N. J.
Navy Blue . . . Gray . . . . . Moravian College, Pa.

Navy Blue . . .	Silver Gray	Hood College, Md.
Purple Navy . .	Gray . . .	Polytechnic Institute of Brooklyn, N. Y.
Royal Blue . .	Gray . .	Rochester Institute of Technology, N. Y.
Yale Blue . . .	Silver Gray	Upsala College, N. J.

2exx. *Blue top with Chevron and different color bottom*

Top	Chevron	Bottom	Institution
Blue . .	.White . .	.Burnt Orange .	Sam Houston State Teachers College, Tex.

2fa. *Orange with Black Chevron*

Field	Chevron	Institution
Burnt Orange . .	Black . . .	Pacific, University of the, Calif.
Burnt Orange . .	Black . . .	West Virginia Wesleyan College, Va.
Orange . . .	Black	Anderson College, Ind.
Orange . . .	Black	Findlay College, Ohio
Orange . . .	Black	Georgetown College, Ky.
Orange . . .	Black	Hendrix College, Ark.
Orange . . .	Black . . .	Idaho State College, Idaho
Orange . . .	Black . . .	Jamestown College, N. Dak.
Orange . . .	Black .	Northwest, Nazarene College, Idaho
Orange . . .	Black . . .	Occidental College, Calif.
Orange . . .	Black . .	Oklahoma State University, Okla.
Orange . . .	Black . . .	Paterson State College, N. J.
Orange . . .	Black . . .	Princeton University, N. J.
Orange . . .	Black . . .	Superior State College, Wis.
Orange . . .	Black	Union College, Ky.
Orange . . .	Black	Waynesburg College, Pa.
Orange . . .	Black .	Western Montana College of Education, Mont.

2fb. *Orange with White or Silver Chevron*

Orange	White . .	California Institute of Technology, Calif.
Orange	White	Texas, University of, Tex.

2fd. *Orange with Red Chevron*

Orange	Maroon . .	Virginia Polytechnic Institute, Va.

2fe. *Orange with Blue Chevron*

Burnt Orange .	Royal Blue	Auburn University, Ala.
Burnt Orange .	Royal Blue	Northland College, Wis.
Orange . . .	Blue	Florida, University of, Fla.
Orange . . .	Navy Blue	Louisiana College, La.
Orange . . .	Royal Blue . . .	Macalester College, Minn.
Orange . . .	Yale Blue	Bucknell University, Pa.

2fh. *Orange with Green Chevron*

Orange . . . . Green . . . Florida A and M University, Fla.

2fi. *Orange with Brown Chevron*

Burnt Orange . . Brown . . Bowling Green State University, Ohio

2fxx. *Orange top with Chevron and different color bottom*

Top	Chevron	Bottom	Institution
Orange .	White .	Green . .	Miami, University of, Fla.

2gb. *Purple with White or Silver Chevron*

Field	Chevron	Institution
Deep Purple . .	White	Mills College of Education, N. Y.
Deep Violet . .	White	Spring Hill College, Ala.
Lavender . .	White	Hunter College, N. Y.
Medium Purple .	White	Chatham College, Pa.
Purple . . .	Cream	Tarkio College, Mo.
Purple . . .	White . . .	Abilene Christian College, Tex.
Purple . . .	White . . .	Agnes Scott College, Ga.
Purple . . .	White . . .	Amherst College, Mass.
Purple . . .	White . . .	Annhurst College, Conn.
Purple . . .	White	Asbury College, Ky.
Purple . . .	White . . .	Biblical Sem in New York, N. Y.
Purple . . .	White	Bluffton College, Ohio
Purple . . .	White . . .	Bridgeport, University of, Conn.
Purple . . .	White . .	Evangelical Theological Seminary, Ill.
Purple . . .	White . . .	Grand Canyon College, Ariz.
Purple . . .	White . . .	High Point College, N. C.
Purple . . .	White . . .	Immaculate Heart College, Calif.
Purple . . .	White . . .	Kentucky Wesleyan College, Ky.
Purple . . .	White .	New Mexico Highlands University, N. Mex.
Purple . . .	White . .	Newton Theological Institution, Mass.
Purple . . .	White . . .	Niagara University, N. Y.
Purple . . .	White . .	Osteopathic Medicine and Surgery, College of, Iowa
Purple . . .	White . . .	Portland, University of, Oreg.
Purple . . .	White	Rockford College, Ill.
Purple . . .	White . .	Stephen F. Austin State College, Tex.
Purple . . .	White . .	Trevecca Nazarene College, Tenn.
Purple . . .	White	Venard College, Iowa
Purple . . .	White . .	Wesley Theological Seminary, D. C.
Purple . . .	White . . .	Whitewater St College, Wis.
Purple . . .	White	Wiley College, Tex.
Purple . . .	White . . .	Winona State College, Minn.
Royal Purple . .	White	Mount Union College, Ohio

Royal Purple	White	Scranton, University of, Pa.
Violet	White	Nyack Missionary College, N. Y.

2gc. *Purple with Yellow or Gold Chevron*

Purple	Bright Gold	Barrington College, R. I.
Purple	Bright Gold	Whittier College, Calif.
Purple	Gold	Albany College of Education at, N. Y. (SUNY)
Purple	Gold	Berkeley Baptist Divinity School, Calif.
Purple	Gold	Black Hills Teachers College, S. D.
Purple	Gold	Carver School of Missions and Social Work, Ky.
Purple	Gold	Chicago College of Chiropody, Ill.
Purple	Gold	Chicago Medical School, Ill.
Purple	Gold	Cincinnati Bible Seminary, Ohio
Purple	Gold	David Lipscomb College, Tenn.
Purple	Gold	East Carolina College, N. C.
Purple	Gold	Florence State College, Ala.
Purple	Gold	Holy Names College, Wash.
Purple	Gold	Idaho, College of, Idaho
Purple	Gold	Kansas City College of Osteopathy and Surgery, Mo.
Purple	Gold	Mankato State College, Minn.
Purple	Gold	Mt. St. Mary's College, Calif.
Purple	Gold	New Mexico Western College, N. Mex. (Unoff)
Purple	Gold	New Orleans Baptist Theo Sem, La.
Purple	Gold	New York, University of the State of (Regents), N. Y.
Purple	Gold	Northwestern University, Ill.
Purple	Gold	Olivet Nazarene College, Ill.
Purple	Gold	Ricker College, Maine
Purple	Gold	Rider College, N. J.
Purple	Gold	San Francisco State College, Calif.
Purple	Gold	Tennessee Polytechnic Institute, Tenn.
Purple	Gold	Trinity College, D. C.
Purple	Gold	West Chester State College, Pa.
Purple	Gold	Western Illinois University, Ill.
Purple	Gold	Westminster College, Utah
Purple	Old Gold	Knox College, Ill.
Purple	Old Gold	Shelton College, N. J.
Purple	Old Gold	Tennessee Polytechnic Inst, Tenn.
Purple	Yellow	Dallas Theo Sem, Tex.
Royal Purple	Gold	Westminster Choir C, N. J.
Royal Purple	Old Gold	Carroll College, Mont.
Royal Purple	Old Gold	Lemoyne College, Tenn.
Royal Purple	Old Gold	St. Catherine, College of, Minn.

2gd. *Purple with Red Chevron*

Mauve	Crimson . . .	Textile Technology, Inst of, Va.
Purple	Cardinal . . .	Linfield College, Oreg.

2gf. *Purple with Orange Chevron*

Northwestern Purple	Burnt Orange . . .	Clemson College, S. C.

2gg. *Purple with Purple Chevron*

Purple	Lavender	Wesleyan College, Ga.

2gj. *Purple with Gray Chevron*

Purple Navy . .	Gray . .	Polytechnic Institute at Brooklyn, N. Y.
Purple	Gray	St. Thomas, College of, Minn.

2gxx. *Purple top with Chevron and different color bottom*

Top	Chevron	Bottom	Institution
Royal Purple	Silver Grey	Education Blue .	Arkansas St Tchers C, Ark.

2ha. *Green with Black Chevron*

Field	Chevron	Institution
Nile Green . . .	Black	Central College, Mo.

2hb. *Green with White Chevron*

Dark Green . . .	White	Chicago Teachers College, Ill.
Dark Green . . .	White	Johnson Teachers College, Vt.
Dartmouth Green .	White . . .	Plymouth Teachers College, N. H.
Dartmouth Green .	White	Wagner College, N. Y.
Emerald Green . .	White . .	New School for Social Research, N. Y.
Emerald Green . .	White	Stetson University, Fla.
Forest Green . .	White . .	Gorham State Teachers College, Maine
Forest Green . .	White . . .	Pan American College, Tex.
Green	Silver .	Eastern New Mexico University, N. Mex.
Green	White .	Andrews University, Mich. (Bach. only) Unofficial
Green	White . .	Arkansas A and M College, Ark.
Green	White . . .	Bethany College, W. Va.
Green	White . .	Eastern Michigan University, Mich.
Green	White .	Northwest Missouri State College, Mo.
Green	White .	Presbyterian School of Christian Education, Va.
Green	White .	Scaritt College for Christian Workers, Tenn.
Green	White . .	Western Evangelical Seminary, Oreg.
Hunter Green . .	White .	Michigan State University, Mich. (Unofficial)
Kelly Green . .	White . . .	Adams State College, Colo.
Kelly Green . .	White . . .	Marshall University, W. Va.

Kelly Green .	.	.	White	.	.	.	.	North Texas, University of, Tex.
Kelly Green .	.	.	White	.	.	.	.	Slippery Rock State College, Pa.
Kelly Green .	.	.	White	.	.	.	.	Wilmington College, Ohio
Myrtle Green	.	.	White	.	.	.	.	Medical College of Virginia, Va.
Olive Green .	.	.	White	.	.	.	.	Lake Erie College, Ohio
Veridian Green	.	.	White	.	.	.	.	Roosevelt University, Ill.

2hc. *Green with Yellow or Gold Chevron*

Dartmouth Green	.	Gold	.	.	.	.	.	Marlboro College, Vt.
Emerald Green .	.	Gold	.	Brockport College of Education (SUNY), N. Y.
Forest Green	.	Gold	.	.	St. Bernadine of Siena College, N. Y.
Forest Green	.	Yellow Gold	.	.	.	St. Vincent College, Pa.
Forest Green	.	Old Gold	.	.	.	Wayne State University, Mich.
Green	.	.	.	Gold	.	.	.	.	Baylor University, Tex.
Green	.	.	.	Gold	.	.	.	.	Jersey City State College, N. J.
Green	.	.	.	Gold	.	.	.	.	Keuka College, N. Y.
Green	.	.	.	Gold	.	.	.	.	Lesley College, Mass.
Green	.	.	.	Gold	.	.	.	Oklahoma Baptist University, Okla.
Green	.	.	.	Gold	.	.	.	.	Tiffin University, Ohio
Green	.	.	.	Gold	.	.	.	Vermont, University of, Vt.
Hunter Green	.	Bright Gold	.	Duchesne College of the Sacred Heart, Nebr.
Kelly Green .	.	Gold	.	.	.	.	Pasadena College, Calif.
Kelly Green .	.	Gold	.	.	San Francisco, University of, Calif.
Kelly Green .	.	Yellow Gold	.	.	Humboldt State College, Calif.
Lincoln Green	.	Gold	.	.	Drew University, N. J. (B.A. only)
Medium Green	.	Yellow	.	.	.	(Boston) State College, Mass.
Myrtle Green	.	Yellow Gold	.	.	.	Concordia Seminary, Mo.
Olive Green .	.	Old Gold	.	.	Western Maryland College, Md.

2hd. *Green with Red Chevron*

Apple Green	.	Scarlet	.	.	.	.	Huntington College, Ind.
Dark Green .	.	Pale Pink	.	.	.	Sweet Briar College, Va.
Green	.	.	.	Red	.	.	.	Washington University, Mo.

2he. *Green with Blue Chevron*

| Olive Green . | . | Light Blue | . | . | . | Tulane University, La. |

2hf. *Green with Orange Chevron*

| Forest Green | . | Burnt Orange | . | . | Walla Walla College, Wash. |

2hj. *Green with Gray Chevron*

| Green | . | . | . | Gray | . | . | . | . | Loyola College, Md. |

2hxx. *Green top with Chevron and different color bottom*

Top	Chevron	Bottom	Institution
Green	Gold	White	Pacific Bible Seminary, Calif.
Piper Green	Gold	Bright Green	Hollins College, Va.
Bottle Green	U.S. Army Silver Gray	Gold	William and Mary, C of, Va.

2ib. *Brown with White or Silver Chevron*

Field	Chevron	Institution
Brown	White	St. Bonaventure University, N. Y. (Doctors only)

2ic. *Brown with Yellow or Gold Chevron*

Cocoa Brown	Live Medium Gold	Woman's College of Georgia, Ga.
Brown	Gold	Baldwin-Wallace College, Ohio
Brown	Gold	Cleveland-Marshall Law School, Ohio
Brown	Gold	Regis College, Colo.
Brown	Yellow	Wyoming, University of, Wyo.
Seal Brown	Old Gold	Western Michigan University, Mich.

2id. *Brown with Red Chevron*

Seal Brown	Cardinal	Brown University, R. I.

2ie. *Brown with Blue Chevron*

Brown	Blue	Tufts College, Mass.
Medium Brown	Light Blue	Newcomb College, La.

2jd. *Gray with Red Chevron*

Gray	Crimson	Loyola University of Los Angeles, Calif.
Gray	Crimson	St. Xavier College, Ill.
Gray	Crimson	Worcester Polytechnic Institute, Mass.
Gray	Harvard Crimson	Southern California School of Theology, Calif.
Gray	Red	Hamline University, Minn.
Gray	Red	Stevens Institute of Technology, N. J.
Gray	Rose	Viterbo College, Wis.
Silver Gray	Cherry Red	New Mexico, University of, N. Mex.
Silver Gray	Scarlet	Christian Theo Sem, Ind.
Silver Gray	Scarlet	Woman's Medical College of Pennsylvania, Pa.
Silver Gray	Spectrum Red (Wide)	Georgia State College of Business Administration, Ga.

2je. *Gray with Blue Chevron*

Confederate Gray	Union Blue	Georgetown University, D. C.
Pearl Gray	Light Blue	Cincinnati College Conservatory of Music, Ohio

2jxx. *Gray top with Chevron and different color bottom*

Top	Chevron	Bottom	Institution
Silver Gray	Black	Red	Barry College, Fla.
Gray	Red	Purple	Seabury Western Theo Sem, Ill.

3be. *White with Blue Chevron Reversed*

Field	Chevron Reversed	Institution
White	Royal Blue	Saint Mary of the Plains College, Kans.

3ca. *Yellow or Gold with Black Chevron Reversed*

Spanish Yellow	Black	Mississippi Southern College, Miss.

3cb. *Yellow or Gold with White Chevron Reversed*

Gold	White	Mt. Angel Seminary, Oreg.

3cd. *Yellow or Gold with Red Chevron Reversed*

Gold	Crimson	New York Medical College, N. Y.

3da. *Red with Black Chevron Reversed*

Cardinal	Black	William Jewell College, Mo.
Red	Black	Whitworth College, Wash.

3db. *Red with White Chevron Reversed*

Cardinal	White	Albright College, Pa.
Cardinal, Dark	White	Chadron State Teachers College, Nebr.
Maroon	Cream	Alma College, Mich.
Maroon	White	Morningside College, Iowa
Red	White	Houston, University of, Tex.
Red	White	Saint Benedict, College of, Minn.

3dc. *Red with Yellow or Gold Chevron Reversed*

Crimson	Gold	Faith Theological Seminary, Pa.
Scarlet	Gold	Central State College, Ohio

3de. *Red with Blue Chevron Reversed*

Garnet	Turquoise	George Peabody C for Teachers, Tenn. (MA., Ph.D.)
Gules	Pale Azure	Duquesne University, Pa.

3dj. *Red with Gray Chevron Reversed*

Cardinal	Silver Gray	Massachusetts Institute of Tech., Mass.
Maroon	Silver Gray	Aquinas College, Mich.
Rose	Gray	Vassar College, N. Y.

3eb. *Blue with White Chevron Reversed*

Light Blue	White	Jewish Studies, College of, Ill.
Blue	White	Free Will Baptist Bible College, Tenn.
Navy Blue	White	North Georgia College, Ga.
Royal Blue	White	Hampton Institute, Va.

3ec. *Blue with Yellow or Gold Chevron Reversed*

Dark Blue	Gold	Trenton State College, N. J.
Royal Blue	Goldenrod	Montana State College, Mont.

3ed. *Blue with Red Chevron Reversed*

Navy Blue	Scarlet	Cleary College, Mich.

3ef. *Blue with Orange Chevron Reversed*

Blue	Orange	Gettysburg College, Pa.

3ej. *Blue with Gray Chevron Reversed*

Navy Blue	Cadet Gray	Reformed Episcopal Ch, Theo Sem of, Pa.

3exx. *Blue top with Chevron reversed and different color bottom*

Top	Chevron Rev.	Bottom	Institution
Dark Blue	Gold	Light Blue	College Misericordia, Pa.

3fa. *Orange with Black Chevron Reversed*

Field	Chevron Reversed	Institution
Burnt Orange	Black	East Central State College, Okla.

3gc. *Purple with Yellow or Gold Chevron Reversed*

Purple	Gold	Alabama College, Ala.
Purple	Gold	Bethel College, Tenn.
Purple	Gold	Hardin Simmons University, Tex.
Purple	Gold	Kansas Wesleyan University, Kans.
Purple	Gold	Louisiana State University, La.
Purple	Gold	Southwestern Bible Institute, Tex.
Purple	Gold	Texas College, Tex.

3hb. *Green with White Chevron Reversed*

Emerald Green	White	Sarah Lawrence College, N. Y.
Green	White	Ohio University, Ohio
Kelly Green	White	Northeastern State College, Okla.
Olive Green	White	Salem College, W. Va.

3hc. *Green with Yellow or Gold Chevron Reversed*

Forest Green	Gold	St. Bernadine of Siena College, N. Y.
Olive Green	Gold	Pacific Lutheran Theo Sem, Calif.

3hf. *Green with Orange Chevron Reversed*

Emerald Green .   .   .   Gold Orange .   .   .   .   . LaVerne College, Calif.

3jg. *Gray with Purple Chevron Reversed*

Gray .   .   .   .   Purple .   .   .   .   . Radford College, Va.

3jca. *Gray top with Chevron reversed and different color bottom*

Top	*Chevron Rev.*	*Bottom*	*Institution*
Gray . . .Gold . . .Black .			United States Military Academy, N. Y.

4a. *Black with two Chevrons*

Field	*Chevrons*	*Institution*
Black	Old Gold	Purdue University, Ind.

4b. *White or Silver with two Chevrons*

Silver	Gold	Idaho, University of, Idaho
		(Projected for earned degrees)
White	Red	Talbot Theo Sem, Calif.
White	Scarlet . . .	Southeastern Bible College, Ala.
White	Royal Blue . . .	Dyke College, Ohio
White	Royal Blue . .	St. Mary of the Plains College, Kans.
White	Orange .	Texas Western College, Tex. (Bach. only)

4c. *Yellow or Gold with two Chevrons*

Gold	Black .	Andrews University, Mich. (Grad. degrees)
Old Gold . .	Black	Missouri, University of, Mo.
Light Gold . .	White	Limestone College, S. C.
Golden Yellow .	Royal Blue . . .	Rockefeller Institute, N. Y.
Old Gold . .	Royal Blue	Briar Cliff College, Iowa
Gold	Purple . . .	Chicago Conservatory College, Ill.

4d. *Red with two Chevrons*

Bright Red . . .	Black	Cincinnati, University of, Ohio
Bright Red . .	White	Northern Baptist Theo Sem, Ill.
Carnelian . .	White	Cornell University, N. Y.
Maroon . . .	White	Hastings College, Nebr.
Maroon . . .	White	Seattle Pacific College, Wash.
Red	White	Rio Grande College, Ohio
Scarlet . . .	White .	American University of Beirut, Lebanon
Burgundy . . .	Gold .	Los Angeles Conservatory of Music, Calif.
Cardinal . . .	Mikado Yellow . . .	Oberlin College, Ohio
Crimson . . .	Gold	Regis College, Mass.
Scarlet . . .	Old Gold . .	Central Baptist Seminary, Kans.
Maroon . . .	Orange	Susquehanna University, Pa.

4e. *Blue with two Chevrons*

Columbia Blue . .	White . . .	North Carolina, University of, N. C.
(Light Blue)		
Navy Blue . . .	White	Villanova University, Pa.
Navy Blue . . .	White	Xavier University, Ohio
Royal Blue . . .	White	Trinity College, Ill.
Light Blue . . .	Yellow . . .	South Dakota State College, S. Dak.
Navy Blue . . .	Orange	Illinois, University of, Ill.

4f. *Orange with two Chevrons*

Deep Orange . .	Dark Blue	Wheaton College, Ill.

4g. *Purple with two Chevrons*

Purple (Medium) .	White	Capital University, Ohio
Purple	White	Kansas State University, Kansas
Purple	White . . .	Western Ontario, University of, Ont.
Royal Purple . .	White	McKendree College, Ill.
Purple	Gold	Alfred University, N. Y.
Purple	Gold	Western Carolina College, N. C.
Royal Purple . .	Gold	St. Scholastica, College of, Minn.
Royal Purple . .	Lemon Gold	Albion College, Mich.

4h. *Green with two Chevrons*

Emerald Green . .	White	Hawaii, University of, Hawaii
Kelly Green . . .	Yellow Gold .	California St. Polytechnic College, Calif.

4i. *Brown with two Chevrons*

Brown	White .	St. Bonaventure University, N. Y. (Bach. only)

4j. *Gray with two Chevrons*

Gray	Crimson	Guilford College, N. C.
Gray	Scarlet	Drury College, Mo.

4xx. *Two Chevrons of different colors* (Field shows between chevrons)

White	Purple (upper), Gold (lower) .	Clarke College, Iowa

5. *Two Chevrons Reversed* (Field shows between chevrons)

Field	*Chevrons Reversed*	*Institution*
Robin's Egg Blue .	White	Bethany Bible College, Calif.
Blue	White . . .	Washington and Lee University, Va.
Royal Blue . . .	Gold . . .	St. Joseph on the Rio Grande, N. Mex.
Medium Blue . .	Silver Gray . . .	Eastern Illinois University, Ill.
Orange	Black	Mercer University, Ga.
Olive Green . . .	Gold	Northern Michigan College, Mich.

6. *Three Chevrons* (Field shows between chevrons)

Field	*Chevrons*	*Institution*
Black	Orange	Wartburg College, Iowa
Gold	Black	Millersville State College, Pa.
Gold	Blue	Jarvis Christian College, Tex.
Gold	Blue	Ladycliff College, N. Y.
Old Gold	Deep Purple	Taylor University, Ind.
Old Gold	Purple	Pittsburgh Theo Sem, Pa.
Old Gold	Kelly Green	Steubenville, College of, Ohio
Maroon	Gold	Shimer College, Ill.
Yale Blue	White	Illinois College, Ill.
Royal Blue	Gold	Fuller Theological Seminary, Calif.
Orange	Black	Kalamazoo College, Mich.
Purple	White	Cornell College, Iowa
Red	Black, Orange, Black	Heidelberg College, Ohio

7. *Three Chevrons Reversed*

Field	*Chevrons Reversed*	*Institution*
White	Red (varying width)	Cranbrook Academy of Art, Mich.

8. *Double Chevron* (does not show field between chevrons)

Field	*Chevrons*	*Institution*
Red	White and Gold	Kansas City Bible College, Mo.
Old Gold	Crimson and Royal Blue	Tulsa, University of, Okla.

10. *Triple Chevrons* (Does not show field between chevrons)

Field	*Chevrons*	*Institution*
Royal Blue	White, Seafoam Green, White	Illinois College of Optometry
Pale Blue	Gold, White, Black	St. Mary's Sem and U, Md.

12a. *Per Chevron, Black over another color*

Top	*Bottom*	*Institution*
Black	Princeton Orange	Lewis and Clark C, Oreg.

12b. *Per Chevron, White over another color*

White	Gold	Nazareth College, Ky.
White	Scarlet	Cortland, C of Ed at (SUNY) N. Y.
White	Blue	Brigham Young U, Utah
White	Blue	Westminster College, Pa.
White	Dark Blue	Assumption College, Mass.
White	National Blue	Louisville Presbyterian Theo Sem, Ky.
White	Royal Blue	Austin Presbyterian Theo Sem, Tex.
White	Purple	Niagara U, N. Y. (Obsolete)

12c. *Per Chevron, Gold over another color*

Old Gold	. . .	Black	. . . . Brenau College, Ga.
Old Gold	. . .	Black	. . . . . . Southwestern U, Tex.
Old Gold	. . .	White	. . . . American International C, Mass.
Yellow	. . .	White	. . . . . . Salem College, W. Va.
Gold	. . .	Crimson	. . . . . . Coe College, Iowa
Old Gold	. . .	Cardinal	. . . . . Iowa State U, Iowa
Old Gold	. . .	Scarlet	. . . San Diego C for Women, Calif.
Lemon	. . .	Royal Blue	. . . . Bethany College, Kans.
Old Gold	. . .	Navy Blue	. . West Virginia University, W. Va.
Old Gold	. . .	Royal Blue	. . . . Augustana College, S. D.
Old Gold	. . .	Royal Blue	. Chattanooga, University of, Tenn. (Honoraries)
Old Gold	. . .	Royal Blue	. . Notre Dame, University of, Ind.
Gold	. . .	Purple	. . . . . Elmira College, N. Y.
Gold	. . .	Purple	. . . . . Madison College, Va.
Old Gold	. . .	Olive Green	. . . Chicago Lutheran Theo Sem, Ill.
Gold	. . .	Brown	. . Chestnut Hill College of the Sisters of St. Joseph, Pa.

12d. *Per Chevron, Red over another color*

Bright Red	. . .	Black	. . . . Georgia, University of, Ga.
Cardinal	. . .	Black	. . . Southwestern at Memphis, Tenn.
Red	. . . .	Black	. . . . . Lake Forest College, Ill.
Red	. . . .	Black	. . Washington and Jefferson College, Pa.
Cardinal	. . .	White	. . . . . Detroit University, Mich.
Cardinal	. . .	White	. . . . Santa Clara University, Calif.
Red	. . . .	White	. . . . . St. Martin's College, Wash.
Scarlet	. . .	Cream	. . . Nebraska, University of, Nebr.
Crimson	. . .	Gold	. . . . . Seton Hill College, Pa.
Red	. . . .	Blue	. . . . Sacred Heart College, Kans.
Crimson	. . .	Silver Gray	. Washington State University, Wash.

12e. *Per Chevron, Blue over another color*

Light Blue	. . .	White	. . . . Creighton University, Nebr.
Light Blue	. . .	White	. Mt. Saint Mary's College, Md. (Honoraries)
(Royal) Blue	. .	White	. . New Hampshire, University of, N. H.
Light Blue	. . .	White	. . . New Rochelle, College at, N. Y.
Royal Blue	. . .	White	. . . Villa Madonna College, Ky.
Blue	. . . .	Gold	. . . . . Emmanuel College, Mass.
Blue	. . . .	Gold	. Texas College of Arts and Industries, Tex.
Yale Blue	. . .	Gold	. . . . . Rollins College, Fla.
Light Navy	. . .	Silver Gray	. . Colorado School of Mines, Colo.
Yale Blue	. . .	Gray	. . . . . Colby College, Maine

12f. *Per Chevron, Orange over another color*

Orange	White	Texas Western College, Tex. (Masters only)
Orange	Blue	Hope College, Mich.
Orange	Navy Blue	Morgan State College, Md.
Orange	Purple	Hobart College, N. Y.

12g. *Per Chevron, Purple over another color*

Purple	Gold	Loras College, Iowa
Purple	Gold	Washington, University of, Wash.
Royal Purple	Old Gold	Prairie View Agricultural College, Tex.

12h. *Per Chevron, Green over another color*

Green	White	Illinois Wesleyan University, Ill.
Kelly Green	White	Bimidji State College, Minn.
Kelly Green	Old Gold	Missouri School of Religion, Mo.

12i. *Per Chevron, Brown over another color*

Brown	White	Case Institute of Technology, Ohio
Brown	White	St. Bonaventure University, N. Y. (Masters only)

14. *Single Bar*

Field	*Bar*	*Institution*
Silver	Gold	Idaho, University of, Idaho (Honoraries)
White	Purple	Iowa Wesleyan College, Iowa
Gold	White	Catholic University of America, D. C. (Unofficial)
Medium Blue	White	Webb Institute of Naval Arch., N. Y.
Purple	White	Berkshire Christian College, Mass.

17. *Double Bar*

Field	*Bars*	*Institution*
Copper	Silver-Gold	Montana State University, Mont.

19. *Per Bar*

Top	*Bottom*	*Institution*
Yellow Gold	White	Towson State Teachers College, Md.
Gold	Cardinal Red	St. John Fisher College, N. Y.
Gold	Royal Blue	Pace College, N. Y.
California Gold	Royal Blue	Western Theological Seminary, Mich.
Peacock Blue	White	Upper Iowa University, Iowa
Purple	Gold	Emerson College, Mass.

23. *Per Pale*

Left	*Right*	*Institution*
Black	Orange	Midland College, Nebr.
Bright Gold . . .	Kelly Green .	Northwestern Lutheran Theo Sem, Minn.
Blue	White .	Our Lady of the Snows Scholasticate, Miss.
Blue	Gold . . .	Detroit Institute of Musical Art, Mich.

23-2. *Per Pale with Chevron*

Left	*Right*	*Chevron*	*Institution*
White	Green .	Yellow . . .	St. Norbert College, Wis.

24. *Cross*

Field	*Cross*	*Institution*
White	Red	Divinity School in Philadelphia, Pa.

30. *Tartans*

"Carnegie Tartan" . . . . . . Carnegie Institute of Technology, Pa.

(3 Blue, ½ Red, ½ Blue, 2 Red, 6 Blue, ½ Red, 6 Black, 6 Green, 2 Red, ½ Green, ½ Red, 2 Green, 1 Yellow. This is crossed with the same except that Blue is substituted for Black. This description comes from a sample furnished by the institute.)

Clergy Tartan . . Covenant College and Covenant Theological Seminary, Mo.

(1 Green, 1 Black, 1 Green, 3 Blue, 3 Black, 1 Green, 3 Black, 1 Green, 2 Blue, 1 Green, 3 Blue, 1 Green. This description comes from a sample furnished by the college.)

99. *Code Hoods Not in Other Patterns*

Light Blue charged with Gold circle	American Conservatory, Ill.
Sage Green with Deep V-shaped Silver Stripe . . .	Scripps College, Calif.
Gray, Gold, and Black vertical divisions from inside out .	U. S. Military Academy, New York

100. *Non-Code Hoods*

ART INSTITUTE OF CHICAGO, ILL.

Black hood, trimmed with two bands starting at the neck and overlapping at the back. Right band is Sand colored with darker stripes. Left band is alternately Turquoise and Silver Gray.

BERKELEY DIVINITY SCHOOL, CONN.

Literate's hood. Black stuff on silk with one-inch edging of Scarlet silk.
S.T.B. Black faille. Oxford shape, three feet long, lined Scarlet with one-inch Scarlet facing on rounded edge of hood.

S.T.M. Black faille. Oxford shape, three feet six inches long lined Scarlet with one-inch Scarlet facing on rounded edge of hood. Red cord trim on straight edge of hood.

S.T.D. Black silk American intercollegiate style, lined Scarlet with one-inch Scarlet facing on rounded edge.

CHURCH DIVINITY SCHOOL OF THE PACIFIC, CALIF.

All hoods are lined in Old Gold.
B.D. Black, Piped Red
S.T.M. Black, Piped Red
D.D. and S.T.D. Red, Piped Red
L.H.D. Black, Piped White
D.C.L. Black, Piped Red and Purple

GENERAL THEOLOGICAL SEMINARY, N. Y.

S.T.B. Black, lined Purple
S.T.M. Black, lined Scarlet
S.T.D. Scarlet, lined Purple

HARVARD UNIVERSITY, MASS.

All hoods are Black, lined Crimson. They differ only in length which for the bachelors is three feet; masters, three and one half feet; and doctors, four feet. No indication of the faculty is worn on the hood as it is shown on the lapel of the gown.

NASHOTA HOUSE, WIS.

Graduates and doctors wear a hood of a special Nashota pattern.
Bachelors and Masters wear the code pattern hood.
Graduate. Black stuff, lined with black stuff, bordered with Red Purple silk and piped Scarlet.
B.D. Red Purple stuff lined with Scarlet silk
S.T.M. Red Purple silk, lined with Scarlet silk
D.D. As S.T.M., but in Nashota pattern
S.T.D. As S.T.M., but in Nashota pattern and with Dark Blue Chevron
Th.D. As S.T.M., but in Nashota pattern and with Dark Blue double Chevron
LL.D. Red Purple silk, lined with Blue Purple silk
D.C.L. As LL.D., but with Scarlet Chevron
Mus.D. Red Purple silk, lined with Pink silk

OHIO COLLEGE OF CHIROPODY

Hoods are not used for earned degrees. Instead a "Collar of Honor" is awarded. It is Kelly Green with two streamers lengthwise Royal Blue and Gold hanging down the back.

OTIS ART INSTITUTE, CALIF.

Dark Brown Velvet, Sky Blue satin lining.

St. John's College, Md.

B.A. Black stuff, lined with Black silk, edged on the inside with a narrow border of Old Gold silk.

B.S. As above, edged on the inside with Garnet silk.

M.A. Black silk with a full lining of Old Gold faille silk.

Ph.D. Scarlet cloth with a full lining of Pale Yellow faille silk.

L.H.D. Scarlet cloth with a full lining of Old Gold faille silk.

LL.D. Scarlet cloth, with a full lining of Garnet faille silk.

D.D. Scarlet cloth with a full lining of White faille silk.

ScD. Scarlet cloth with a full lining of Cardinal faille silk.

Mus.D. Scarlet cloth with a full lining of Pink faille silk.

Tougaloo Southern Christian College, Miss.

Royal Blue hood lined Crimson.

Trinity College, Conn.

All Trinity College hoods are Oxford cut except D.D. which is Cambridge cut.

B.A. Black stuff edged with Palatinate Purple silk.

B.S. Black stuff, edged with Light Blue silk.

Litt.B. Black stuff, edged with Russet Brown silk.

B.D. Black silk, edged with Scarlet silk.

LL.B. Black silk, edged with Dark Blue silk.

Mus.B. Black silk, edged with Pink silk.

M.A. Black silk, edged with Palatinate Purple silk.

M.S. Black cloth, lined with Light Blue silk.

D.D. Scarlet cloth, lined with Black silk.

Litt.D. Scarlet silk, lined with Russet Brown silk.

LL.D. Scarlet silk, lined with Dark Blue silk.

D.C.L. Crimson silk, lined with Black silk.

Mus.D. White silk, lined with Pink silk.

Ph.D. Black silk, lined with Purple silk.

M.D. Scarlet silk, lined with Maroon silk.

Sc.D. Black silk, lined with Light Blue silk.

Mus.M. Black silk, lined with Pink silk.

D.P.H. Black cloth, lined with Salmon-Pink silk.

L.H.D. Scarlet silk, lined with Purple silk.

Academic Processions

Most academic ceremonies begin and end with an academic procession. While this is essentially a simple thing, a little explanation is in order. It is, of course, a descendant of clerical procession. The churches, particularly the Roman Catholic, have had centuries to work out the details to provide maximum dignity and impressiveness. It seems to be a safe rule that when one is in doubt he should follow the clerical pattern.

The procession is formed in ranks of two except where it is desired to single out an individual, for example the person to be inaugurated, he will walk alone. All participants are attired in the costume appropriate to their degrees. There are three exceptions to this. A candidate for a degree to be awarded at the ceremony will, if individual hooding is practiced, appear in cap and gown, but without the hood. The second exception is that in some universities marshals appear in a costume pertaining to their office, rather than to their degrees. The design of this attire is an individual matter for the schools since the Intercollegiate Code does not prescribe it. Finally, military personnel, such as professors of military science, and members of religious orders with distinctive habits will omit academic regalia entirely.

A few schools by statute or custom have a civil dignitary lead the procession. Others, particularly very old institutions follow the British pattern and have a mace in the hands of a bearer lead the formation for all functions. In the absence of either of these it is customary to have the marshal or chief marshal at the head. The marshal usually carries a baton, simple or elaborate, as a badge of office.

Color guards are common and follow the lead element. A word of caution is necessary here. Academic costume is unsuitable for color guards, particularly in outdoor ceremonies. Not only do the necessary straps and sockets confine what should be flowing garments, but there is a very practical objection. A slight breeze will give the bearers enough to do in controlling the colors without having to simultaneously keep the mortarboard and gown in place. It is better to have the flags carried by men in uniform, from the R.O.T.C. if there is one. If it is desired to have students in civilian dress act as guards, dark suits may be worn without any loss of dignity.

If the ceremony is for commencement purposes the next element is that of candidates for degrees. They are arranged in the order in which the degrees will be bestowed. Obviously undergraduate degrees will precede graduate ones and among the latter doctorates will follow masters' degrees. A more difficult problem is raised when it is desired to assign a precedence based on the faculty in which the degree is awarded. Now that divinity and law are recognized as species of graduate or professional faculties, the Bachelor of Arts has emerged as the senior undergraduate title. Probably the Bachelor of Science takes next place unless the Bachelor of Philosophy or Bachelor of Letters degrees are awarded. Beyond this clear cut rules of precedence are lacking. Some schools avoid the issue by awarding degrees in order of the first time they were granted. It is a simpler solution to the problem than trying to evaluate the prestige of Business Administration, Education, Agriculture, Engineering and the like.

Whatever solution is used for the problem of precedence of the degrees, each senior should top off his academic costume with a tassel of the color appropriate to the degree he is to receive. While it may be to the advantage of the costume supplier to simply pack up black tassels, the procession gains when each group of candidates wears a different color tassel identifying the fields of study. This is particularly true when the college grants two or more degrees.

The problem of precedence also occurs with the graduate degrees. Only one thing is clear. The Doctor of Philosophy degree takes absolute precedence over all other earned ones. From that point on each institution will have to work out its own pattern. In a few areas special problems arise because for some masters' degrees a doctorate is a prerequisite, e.g. the M.D. for the M.P.H.

Next in order after the candidates is the faculty. This is usually arranged by rank with the lowest grade first followed by the higher ones. Within each rank the order is that of length of service, newest man first. A few institutions, particularly teachers' colleges with a rankless faculty and those which have only recently granted rank, arrange their faculty strictly by length of service.

In the procession for a ceremony of great consequence, such as an inauguration of a new president of the institution or a bicentennial, to which other universities and learned societies have sent delegates, a separate division is formed. It consists of two parts. The first consists of representatives of the learned societies arranged in inverse order of their founding. Following them are the official delegates of other colleges and universities, again in inverse order of the founding of their institutions. (For convenience the dates for the institutions are given in this book in the table of hoods.)

The final division of the procession is the platform party. It may be arranged to suit the convenience of the institution and the seating arrangements. It should be remembered, however, that the last position is the place of honor and the order of march should reflect that.

In any academic procession it should be noted that dignity is the essence, not military precision. Therefore emphasis on keeping step is out of place. If the marchers fall into step because of the cadence of the music, so much the better, but nothing is really lost if one participant steps out with his right foot while others are on the left. More is lost in trying to get a well drilled team than is gained.

The foregoing description is that of the traditional pattern and order. The 1959 Committee of the American Council on Education describes the procession in the other order, that is, the highest element first and then the lower elements. It adds that sometimes the reverse, i.e. the one just described, is used. In either case the recessional is in the high to low order.

The Commencement Ceremony

The increased size of graduating classes in recent years has required so much time for the actual awarding of degrees that the traditional salutatory and valedictory addresses have almost everywhere been crowded out of the commencement program. If it is desired to reintroduce them, they can be placed at the beginning of the ceremony after the invocation and at the end immediately preceding the benediction.

As thus reduced in content the commencement program today consists primarily of an invocation, a commencement address, the awarding of earned degrees, the awarding of honorary degrees, and the benediction. These elements are frequently supplemented by the singing of the National Anthem, the Alma Mater, and approriate hymns. Occasionally a welcome from the alumni to their new members also appears on the program.

The awarding of degrees is the high point of any commencement, particularly to the recipients. It should therefore be planned carefully to achieve the greatest effect. Ideally every graduate should have his name called in a dignified unhurried manner and should proceed across the stage to receive his diploma and be invested with the hood of his degree. Unfortunately there has been a tendency in recent years to omit the bachelor's hood altogether in the interests of economy. It seems a pity to shave a few dollars from the end of four years of expensive education at the cost of one of the most beautiful symbolic acts in the academic tradition. Time certainly is no objection to using the hooding ceremony. Two, or even three teams, can handle the hoods as rapidly as candidates' names can be called with dignity.

As a practical matter almost everywhere no attempt is made to see that each candidate gets his own diploma at the time he is on the stage. The presiding officer gives him either an empty diploma portfolio or a blank piece of paper. At a more convenient time the document itself is placed in the hands of the recipient.

At the moment the degree is awarded the presiding officer pronounces a formula. It is usually some modification of the form, "By virtue of the Authority vested in me by the State of Blank, I bestow upon you the degree of Blank." Where sheer numbers make individual pronouncements impractical, the presiding officer will often grant the degree to a group prior to the time the first member of it is called on stage. Some universities attempt to use this procedure to retain individual hooding. They ask each candidate to carry his hood to the ceremony and then when the president awards the degree have each man don his own hood. The result is far from satisfactory. Not one man in a hundred can put on his hood with any show of grace. The spectacle of a hundred individuals struggling into the unfamiliar garment is not a pleasing one. If individual hooding by teams cannot be practiced, it is better to have the candidates wear their hoods to the ceremony even though a purist might dispute their right to appear in them prior to the actual awarding of the degree.

The higher degrees are usually awarded individually although in large universities the number of Master's degrees may make it impractical. Often doctoral candidates are presented by their major professors who publicly recommend to the presiding official that So and So be awarded the degree of Doctor of Philosophy. Sometimes the presentation includes mention of the thesis topic. Honorary degrees seem to call for some justification for the college's taking of the step. At any rate, by custom the candidate is usually presented by a member of the faculty who gives an oration about the worthiness of the individual to be honored. Often the whole life of the candidate is reviewed starting with his birth. At the conclusion, in case the point was missed, the president addresses the recipient and reviews the high points of the speech and concludes with the formula of presentation. At the same time he hands over the diploma and the hooding team slips the appropriate hood over the head of the new Doctor of Laws. This is a critical moment from the showmanship standpoint. If the candidate is not warned to remain still until the hooding is complete, he may start to walk off and be brought to an abrupt halt as the neckband tightens up. (There is a story told at the University of Wisconsin, that when this happened, the president's voice came booming over the loudspeaker in what he thought was an inaudible aside, "Rope 'em, darn it, don't throw 'em!")

The inauguration ceremony has as its high points the installation and the inaugural address. The first is a speech, usually by the head of the governing body of the institution, announcing the appointment, a fact well known to all, and charging the new president to perform his new duties faithfully and well. There is often a symbolic delivery of the keys to the college or of a copy of the charter. The president then replies, giving an indication of his appreciation of the honor and some words of praise for the institution and his predecessors. The body of his speech lays down a course of action for his administration. In addition to those elements other activities may include addresses by alumni and civic dignitaries.

PLATE I
1. *Single Color*
WILLIAMS
COLLEGE
Arts

PLATE II
2. *Chevron*
LOYOLA
UNIVERSITY
(ILLINOIS)
Law

PLATE III
3. *Chevron Reversed*
LOUISIANA
STATE UNIV.
Agriculture

PLATE IV
4. *Two Chevrons*
XAVIER
UNIVERSITY
OHIO
*Business
Administration*

PLATE V
5. *Two Chevrons
Reversed*
NORTHERN
MICHIGAN
COLLEGE
Education

PLATE VI
6. *Three Chevrons*
FULLER
THEOLOGICAL
SEMINARY
Theology

PLATE VII
7. *Three Chevrons
Reversed*
Economics

PLATE VIII
8. *Double Chevron*
UNIVERSITY
OF TULSA
Science

PLATE IX
9. *Double Chevron Reversed*
Engineering

PLATE X
10. *Triple Chevron*
ILLINOIS
COLLEGE OF
OPTOMETRY
Optometry

PLATE XI
11. *Triple Chevron Reversed*
Fine Arts

PLATE XII
12. *Party Per Chevron*
WEST VIRGINIA
UNIVERSITY
Dentistry

PLATE XIII
13. *Party Per Chevron Reversed*
Journalism

PLATE XIV
14. *Bar*
CATHOLIC
UNIVERSITY
OF AMERICA
(unofficial)
Philosophy

PLATE XV
15. *Two Bars*
Medicine

PLATE XVI
16. *Three Bars*
Nursing

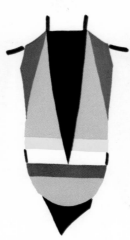

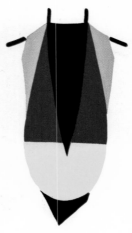

PLATE XVII
17. *Double Bar*
MONTANA
STATE
UNIVERSITY
Forestry

PLATE XVIII
18. *Triple Bar*
Pharmacy

PLATE XIX
19. *Party Per Bar*
EMERSON
COLLEGE
Speech

PLATE XX
20. *Pale*
Physical Education

PLATE XXI
21. *Two Pales*
Podiatry-Chiropody

PLATE XXII
22. *Double Pale*
Public
Administration

PLATE XXIII
23. *Party Per Pale*
DETROIT
INSTITUTE OF
MUSICAL ART
Music

PLATE XXIV
24. *Cross*
DIVINITY
SCHOOL IN
PHILADELPHIA
Theology

PLATE XXV
25. *Party Per Cross*
Social Science

PLATE XXVI
26. *Saltire*
Social Work

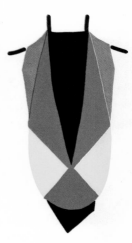

PLATE XXVII
27. *Party Per*
Saltire
Public Health

PLATE XXVIII
28. *Checky*
Veterinary Science

PLATE XXIX
29. *Lozengy*
Arts

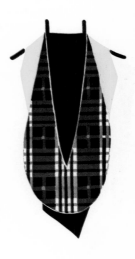

PLATE XXX
30. *Tartan*
Library Science

Academic Seals

American colleges and universities use an institutional seal for authenticating their more important documents. The seal is also frequently used in facsimile on library bookplates, parking permits, college rings, and on student stationery. Oddly enough, it is only infrequently used on official college business stationery, although it sometimes appears as a watermark on the paper.

Most academic seals are circular in shape, although a few schools like Johns Hopkins and the University of Cincinnati use an ancient form which looks like two arcs joined at the top and bottom. Rarely, triangular and square forms are seen. Inside the circle or other border is a legend sometimes in Latin, but more frequently in English, which gives the name of the college and usually the words "Seal of" and the date of founding. Within the legend is a central device often mounted on a shield. This device is intended to be symbolic of the school. Sometimes a view of the campus landmark is shown as in the Oberlin seal. Washington and Lee uses the profiles of its namesakes. Other schools try to display a pictorial representation of the mission of the institution as, for example, Marietta's torch being handed from the older to the younger generation.

The college motto often completes the seal. A collection of these would fill a book by themselves and would probably serve no useful purpose. The mottoes range from Harvard's simple "Veritas" to elaborate restatements of credal positions and are found in English, Latin, Greek and Hebrew.

Almost universally the college seal is found as the central device on the college flag or, more properly, banner.

Academic Flags

The great European universities have their own heraldic insignia duly approved by the proper authorities. In this country, in contrast, each institution adopts its own. This often includes a college flag.

Surprisingly, despite the lack of a central body to prescribe insignia, college flags in the United States are, in general, in good taste and unobjectionable from the heraldic standpoint if certain modifications of the rules are accepted.

The simplest flags are those of colleges which have only one color displayed in their hoods. Williams College, for example, uses a field of Purple in the center of which there is a reproduction of the college seal in gold. Other one-color schools follow the same pattern, arbitrarily choosing a second contrasting color with which to set off the seal. It seems anachronistic to insist on a metal, gold or silver, to set off a design on a colored background simply because that is the rule in classical heraldry. A better rule in the light of modern conditions is to use any combination of colors which are aesthetically pleasing.

Two-color colleges frequently divide the field in half by a horizontal line (party per bar in our terminology) and place the color which predominates in the hood in the top and the subordinate color in the bottom. On this two colored flag is placed the college seal. For the best effect it may be necessary to carry a thin semi-circle of the major color down into the lower half to set off the seal which is usually itself outlined in the minor color.

While the division of the field into two segments by a horizontal line is the usual method, there is no good reason why other divisions may not be used. As a matter of fact where the result of the lateral division is to approximate a national banner, it would be better to use another way of displaying the two colors. A glance at any international flag chart will show various ways of accomplishing the desired effect. It should be noted that merely reproducing the hood as a flag does not give a pleasing result where a chevron is the charge.

Three-color schools follow the same general pattern. The problem of avoiding reproductions of national flags is a little more difficult, but is by no means insoluble.

Heraldic usage and common sense combine to suggest that spelling out the name of the college, its location, and the name of its athletic teams should be avoided. Obviously a flag being carried or whipping from a pole does not lend itself to being read. Where there are many subordinate units of, for instance, a veterans organization, it is probably unavoidable that the flags be lettered. Where, however, each college is free to design its own banner, the wording is undesirable. If one wishes to make a close inspection of the flag, he may discover from the seal which institution it represents. Even in those cases where the inscription is in Latin, a smattering of the language will give him the information.

In procession the college flag is carried to the left of the Stars and Stripes. When the two banners are flown from the facade of a building, the college flag is on the observer's right. In short, the National Flag Code is followed. While there is no code to cover the situation, it seems appropriate to subordinate the college flag to that of the state. This is particularly true in the case of state supported institutions.

Bibliography

Adam, Frank, *Clans, Septs, and Regiments of the Scottish Highlands* rev. by Sir Thomas Innes of Learney, Edinburgh (Johnston) 1955.
>   Contains among other information a description of the Logan System for giving the designs of tartans in words and numbers.

American Council on Education, *American Universities and Colleges,* 8th Edition, 1960, Washington 6, D. C.
>   This edition contains the report of the Committee of the American Council on Education on Academic Costumes and Ceremonies.

Bartholomew, C. A., *Epithetology,* Red Bank, New Jersey (Commercial Press) 1948.
>   An attempt to establish precedence for degrees.

Baty, T., *Academic Colours.* Tokio (Kenkyusha Press) 1934.
>   A discussion of British and Commonwealth universities' hoods. Although the title page carries the publisher as shown, the Kenkyusha Press in a letter dated Nov. 4, 1955, denies having published the book. It is carried in some reference materials as having been published by Simpkins in England.

Carr, H. G., *Flags of the World,* London (Frederick Warne & Co.)
>   A handy compilation of the flags of the world. It shows designs which can be adapted with appropriate color changes to college flags.

Eells, W. C., and Harold A. Haswell, *Academic Degrees,* Washington (U. S. Department of Health, Education and Welfare, Office of Education, OE-54008, Bulletin 1960, No. 28)
>   Excellent work on the degrees offered by American Colleges. Within limits it can be used to establish precedence of degrees since it gives the dates of first award of many of them.

Franklyn, Julian, *Shield and Crest,* New York (Sterling Press) 1960.
>   The best of the modern books on heraldry for the American reader, although its depth of coverage makes it difficult for one interested only in the basic material.

Grosvenor, Gilbert and William J. Showalter, "Flags of the World" *National Geographic Magazine,* Vol. 66, pp. 339, 396, Sept., 1934.
>   Excellent for flags.

Haycraft, F. W., *Degrees and Hoods of the World's Universities and Colleges,* 4th Ed., Cheshunt, Herts (Cheshunt Press Ltd.) 1948.

> An excellent discussion of the origins of academic costume with an index of colors for British and Commonwealth hoods. The American section is inaccurate and out of date. The book is very much worth having.

Moncreiffe, Inan, and Don Pottinger, *Simple Heraldry,* London (Thomas Nelson and Sons Ltd.) 1953.

> For a quick look at heraldic theory and basic designs spiced with humor, it is unexcelled.

Scott-Giles, C. W., *Boutell's Heraldry,* London (Frederick Warne and Co. Ltd.) 1950.

> Modern revision of the old classic.

U. S. Department of Health, Education and Welfare, Office of Education, *Education Directory,* Part 3, 1960-61. Names, locations, and officers of all accredited institutions in the U. S.